MW00942005

SHATTERED DREAMS, BROKEN PIECES

SHATTERED DREAMS, BROKEN PIECES

Donna R. Walton, EdD

Shattered Dreams, Broken Pieces
Copyright © 2017 by Donna R. Walton, EdD. All rights reserved.
No part of this text may be reproduced, transmitted, reverse engi-
neered, decompiled, downloaded, or stored in or introduced into any
information storage and retrieval system, in any form or by any means,
whether electronic or mechanical, now known or hereinafter invented,
without the written permission of Donna R Walton.

Parts of this book were first published in *Amplitude* magazine, an
Amplitude Media Group publication.

Cover design by WorldTech
Cover photograph by Rene´ E. Alston
Other photographs are courtesy of the author unless otherwise noted.

ISBN-10: 1533595151
ISBN-13: 9781533595157

Library of Congress Control Number: 2016909193
CreateSpace Independent Publishing Platform
North Charleston, South Carolina

Photograph by René Alston

Author's Note

Some names, genders, and other identifying
aspects of individuals may have been
changed to protect their privacy. Events
depicted in this narrative are based on the
author's memories and interviews with
others. Since memories differ, the author's
depiction of events may not always agree
with other people's memories. The author
has, however, tried to be as accurate
as possible and regrets any errors.

For my mom,
who always encouraged me to write even when the writer
in me wanted to sing and dance. Thank you for see-
ing in me what I could not see in myself and daring me
to never stop trying.

To my dad, who always questioned my peripatetic nature
but never doubted that where I would end up would be
best for me.

To my sister Lisa for showing me strength and teaching
me how to be a soldier.
To my sisters Margo and Jeanie, who departed this life
far too soon with shattered dreams. May they forever
rest in peace.

Contents

Introduction

"The brave may not live forever, but the cautious do not live at all."

—UNKNOWN

One of my most vivid memories is of a frigid day in January 1976 when I stepped onto a Washington, DC, Metro bus at Lafayette Square and my left leg broke in half. I still recall the screeching siren of the ambulance as it arrived and the murmuring voice of the bus driver complaining that such an event was taking place on his route. The rest of the details are blurred, except for the sound made by people at the sight of something pitiful—a sound resembling the noise made by pigeons and tap shoes. Pain and trauma have a way of clouding one's memory.

I was just 18 years old, and prior to that dreadful day, I had been a self-confident and carefree teenager—someone totally dedicated to becoming a star. I had wanted to dance, sing, and act. I was a young, attractive, smart, and active girl with a full life, and I had thought I had unlimited potential. Like many other teens, I was more than a little self-absorbed. Yes, I really thought I had it going on!

Before that day, I had soul—the kind of soul that funk-and-soul singer James Brown talked about, the kind that made me feel "super bad." But this soul power was no match for what life was about to serve me in the following years as my soul experienced the mother of all beatings.

Another vivid memory is of the day in March 1976 that I woke up in the intensive care unit at the National Institutes of Health (NIH), placed my hand on the bandages that were wrapped around the remains of my left leg, and gave thanks to God that my heart was still beating—that I was still alive!

Nurses hovered; I was hooked up to an IV to "feed" and medicate me; I had a catheter inside me so that I could use the bathroom where I lay; and the monotonous sound of monitoring machines echoed throughout the room. The experience *looked* similar to what I'd seen in movies, but that was where the similarity ended. This experience was real, and it *felt* very different from anything I could have imagined. The surgeons had amputated almost my entire left leg, and

I only had about two inches of femur bone left. It's difficult to explain how it feels to lose a part of oneself. I could already tell that my life was going to change dramatically. I was just 18 years old then, but it was an ordeal that I will never forget.

As I lay there in that hospital bed, grateful for my life, all I wanted to be was alive, well, and free of the memories of how I used to be—free of the thought of everything I had now lost. I was confused and frightened. My faith had been rocked, my confidence shattered.

From that day I woke up in the hospital to this day—this one right here as I'm writing this—I have been revising the story of me. I have had to make new decisions about who I am and what my life and my life's mission are.

Although this process has been difficult at times, it has enabled me to remake a unique person from the shattered dreams and broken pieces of the original me. Today, I am a very different person from the one I was when all of this began. And while the journey from then to now has not been exactly smooth, the gift that I received along the way was the certain knowledge that my potential didn't disappear because I became a one-legged woman.

In the decades following that traumatic experience, I have faced many other crises and will likely face many more as my life continues. I know, how-ever, that each time my life is shattered and broken by trials and tribulations, I can pick up the pieces and put it back together. And while that new life might look different from what it was before, it will likely be better because I had to put in the time and effort to decide how I wanted it to look—to make it *my chosen life*, not one that was simply imposed upon me by circumstances.

■   ■   ■

Losing my leg to cancer was probably the worst crisis I have ever had to face, and although others might con-sider my story a rather dramatic one, the truth is that *no one* escapes life unscarred, unshaken, unshattered, unbroken. *Every one of us* has a story of challenges, of setbacks, of crises, of "failures," of brokenness, of de-feats. Whether these are dramatic and traumatic or just insidious, day-to-day doings that chip away our energy and sap our will, they are inevitable. Some will occur because of external events, and some will occur because of our own weaknesses, mistakes, or "failures." We might face disease, disability, job loss, bankruptcy, divorce, the death of loved ones, or other types of "failure" that makes us feel that we will never recover. In fact, you might be going through one of these terrible crises right now.

It doesn't matter if we are rich or poor; old or young; black, white, brown, yellow, or olive; gay or straight; male or female. It doesn't matter if we are American, Russian, Arab, Chinese, African, or some other racial, ethnic, or national group. It doesn't matter if we are famous or hardly anyone knows our name. Trauma and crisis do not discriminate. They are part of life. You could say that they are "normal." To make it through life with no serious problems would be rare indeed.

And yet, even though such problems are inevitable, we really don't get any training on how to deal with them when they occur. As far as I'm aware, there is no required course in elementary school, middle school, high school, or college called "How to Rebuild a Broken Life." Instead, we get into these crisis situations—our lives get broken into a thousand pieces—and then we have absolutely no idea how to put them back together.

You've probably heard about Humpty Dumpty. If not, one version of his story goes like this:

Humpty Dumpty sat on a wall.
Humpty Dumpty had a great fall.
All the king's horses and all the king's men
Couldn't put Humpty together again.

Unfortunately, many of us believe the basic idea behind this nursery rhyme—the idea that once something is broken, putting it back together is impossible. As a result of this belief, when our lives are shattered by some kind of trauma, we believe that there is no hope to rebuild them, and we simply give up. Some of us become incapacitated and depressed. Others become suicidal.

The reality, however, is that broken lives can be renewed, remade, rebuilt, recycled, reinvented, rebranded. And, in many cases, our new lives can be even better than our old ones—if we know how to deal with the trauma. It's true. Millions of people have proven it. They have done so even when the obstacles blocking their way were like giants and seemed way too large to overcome.

Therefore, we don't have to look at any of these low periods of loss, pain, and difficulty as our final stopping point but merely as one point on a longer journey. This has been true in my own life and in the lives of numerous people I have known personally and have worked with professionally as a certified cognitive behavioral therapist.

■　■　■

This book deals with my life and how I struggled to reinvent myself—to become who and what I wanted to be—after facing serious threats to my life, limb, and dreams.

Readers who don't know me might wonder why they should want to read about a woman they don't know personally. Why should my story interest you? Why should you care?

When journalists report on wars and disasters that take the lives of thousands—maybe even millions—of people, sometimes instead of writing about the thousands or millions, they'll write their articles about one or a few people who personally experienced the devastation. It's too difficult for readers to understand and empathize with thousands or millions of people, but they can understand and empathize with the lone woman searching through piles of rubble to find the body of her child, the lone man who is tortured and murdered by a dictatorial regime, or a child suffering abuse at the hands of a trusted adult. While my story is *my* story, there are many aspects of it that you'll be able to identify with, many areas of it that you will understand, empathize with, and perhaps learn from. While the details of every human being's life and struggles are different, the general themes remain basically the same. The types of problems one person encounters—crisis, shattered dreams, heartrending loss, loneliness, and despair—are common to us all.

I wrote my story because when I lost my leg, there were no positive examples to show me how I could live my life in the midst of shattered dreams and broken pieces and still maintain the original me. There were no stories about how I could thrive in a society that lauds physical attractiveness. There were no television shows, such as *Dancing with the Stars*, or magazines with glossy covers depicting vibrant women with amputation dancing, acting, or leading. There were no wounded warriors walking around with high-tech artificial limbs. There were no Raw Beauty NYC exhibits that showcased photographs of women with various disabilities who represented beauty, sensuality, and empowerment.

I also wrote my story to show that it is possible for us to survive our struggles and reinvent ourselves in the face of life's adversities. I did so in the absence of affirming TV shows, role models, and photo exhibits. I don't say this to brag. My road to reinvention is still evolving. God, I am sure, is not done with me yet.

David Brooks, author of *The Road to Character*, shares his wisdom that "… people can understand themselves only by looking at forces that transcend themselves." For me, that force was amputation. For you, it could be that you were fired from your job. You might be in the depths of despair yourself and wanting to improve your life—to become who and what you want to be—or you might simply not be quite happy with where you are in your life. Whatever your situation is, I hope my story is transformative, fueling you to keep going just when you think you want to quit.

While this book is not intended to be some kind of self-help cookbook or "fix-your-life" guide—since everyone's life is different—it is still my hope that it offers some practical principles and solutions to help you regain resiliency and overcome adversity, crisis, and trauma in your life. And if you, like many people, need it, I hope that my experience and insights can help you pick up the broken pieces of your own life and put them back together to make a new, reinvented life for yourself—one that is a beautiful mosaic of shattered dreams and broken pieces.

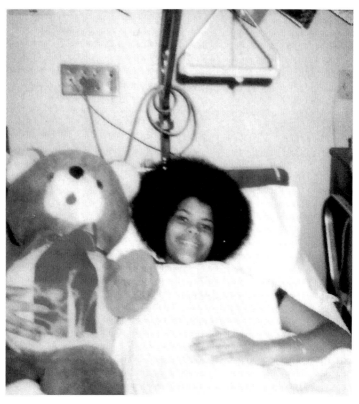

Above: Recovering from amputation at the National Cancer Institute with my favorite get-well teddy bear (circa March 1976).

Broken Pieces

Regret not
the broken pieces,
for nothing
built by humans
is possible
without first
breaking something that already exists
and somehow altering it.

Even a new life,
a new and beautiful mosaic
made of broken pieces
of living human clay,
starts with the broken pieces of
some previous life.

Therefore,
when our lives
are shattered,
sometimes beyond recognition,
we must ask
ourselves
if we should
bemoan our fate
or rather

joyously
pick up the pieces
we want to keep,
paint them in bright and beautiful colors,
and rejoice
at the possibility
of a new
me.

—Donna R. Walton

Part I

Broken Pieces on the Ground

1

The Dream

As I dance high upon the stage—my body squeezed into a red satin dress; my beautiful, long, beige, shapely legs exposed at the sides; my dark brown hair perfectly coiffed; my face adorned with makeup—the spotlight follows me. I sing at the top of my lungs into the microphone I hold in my hand. The applause reverberates throughout the room, and I smile inside, my heart pounding with excitement and joy.

Yes, this was the me I had imagined for years. It was who and what I wanted to be. It was my dream.

Unfortunately, as often happens with dreams, something got in the way before it came true—a little something called reality.

2

Although I had boarded buses hundreds of times over the years, this time, it didn't quite go as planned. As I placed my foot on the steps of the Metro bus at Lafayette Square in Washington, DC, and started to board, my left leg suddenly snapped in half. Yeah, that's right! It broke completely in two.

In that traumatic moment of excruciating pain, my life changed forever.

That was in January 1976.

I was just 18 years old.

3

"No! Not the C Word"

I still recall the screeching siren of the ambulance as it approached the Metro bus that frigid day and then rushed me to The George Washington University Hospital. There, a biopsy was done, and my cancer diagnosis was confirmed. I was then transferred to the National Cancer Institute (NCI), which is part of the National Institutes of Health, where I stayed until sometime in February 1976. I overheard that I had a fracture through a tumor the size of a grapefruit in my knee. Not good.

"The *C* word"—cancer—was front and center, and the doctors wanted to move quickly. The type of bone cancer I had—osteogenic sarcoma—is typically fast moving and extremely deadly. The doctors were proposing amputation and chemotherapy immediately.

My only alternative, according to them: death.

Believe me, the words *cancer*, *amputation*, *chemotherapy*, and *death* are devastating to anyone but especially to a young person full of hopes and dreams. While improved chemotherapy often makes limb-sparing surgery possible and amputation unnecessary today, that was not the case then.

My thoughts were paralyzed at the possibility that I might have to lose my leg and use a wheelchair or an artificial limb.

Nothing in my life up to this point had prepared me for facing such a crisis.

I was terrified of hospitals and scared to death of dying. My spiritual tank quickly went to Empty.

How, I wondered, was I going to deal with such an ordeal?

■ ■ ■

Just a year earlier, I was having a wonderful time. I had always been in love with life, and I believed in sucking the juice out of every moment of it. A wallflower I definitely was not. I was active and highly social, and slowing down was not even a consideration.

Growing up in Washington, DC, I was always "out there," engaged in my world and highly focused on making my mark on it. Without being told, I believed that I had everything I needed to create my own future. Although I was a serious girl, I also had a curious, vivacious, and entrepreneurial spirit. My mission in life seemed to be to know it all and then tell others what I knew. I still recall "holding school" for the neighborhood kids in my basement when I was just 8 years old. In addition, when I was 9, I hosted a backyard carnival for muscular dystrophy, where I raised one hundred dollars! As a born businesswoman, I was always getting involved in things and trying to sell something, even as a child.

I also took my education seriously and excelled academically, although I didn't enjoy junior high school very much. This was partly because my body developed early and I received a lot of unwanted attention from older boys before I was emotionally ready for it.

4

"It Was a Sad Day When Toby Went Away"

"Toby," a 1974 song by popular R&B group The Chi-Lites, is about a young man who went away to college while his girlfriend, Toby, waited for him. But one summer the boyfriend came home, and Toby had died. My boyfriend at the time was touched by the lyrics, and during the summer of 1974, long before my cancer diagnosis and amputation, he nicknamed me Toby when I went away to college. This name stayed with me throughout my undergraduate years.

After graduating high school early (probably because I wanted out of there so badly), I was awarded a scholarship to Point Park College (now Point Park University) in Pittsburgh, Pennsylvania—about 244 miles from home. I had also been accepted by many other undergraduate schools, including a number of highly ranked universities, but Point Park College's financial package sealed the deal and led me to enroll there in the fall of 1974.

While it was scary being so far away from my family and friends when I was just 16, it was also a valuable experience in many ways. I was exposed to people from different backgrounds and made a lot of new friends. Mainly, though, it was exciting to be majoring in performing arts and on my way to fulfilling my dream of one day becoming a great performer.

While I loved college and was enjoying taking classes in my major, there was still a huge problem: I had a boyfriend back in DC, and I missed him terribly. As a result, I was miserable.

So, against my parents' wishes, before the beginning of my sophomore year, I transferred to American University (AU) in Washington, DC, where I began a double major in psychology and elementary and early childhood education. Little did I know at the time that it was all in the master plan for me to take on the study of human behavior so that I could better understand myself and others. In hindsight, it was not a bad decision at all. Although I planned to eventually declare my major in the performing arts, I never got the chance.

Unfortunately, it was in the midst of my seemingly idyllic life in the fall of 1975 that some pain in my left knee, which I had been ignoring for several months, began to command more of my attention. Since I played a lot of tennis, I had naturally assumed that the pain was related to that and had been simply wrapping my knee in bandages and soothing it with BENGAY, an over-the-counter analgesic heat rub used to temporarily relieve pain. At this point, those remedies were no longer solving the problem, and the pain had progressed from an infrequent visitor to a constant and unwelcome companion.

So one day in October, I finally decided to check it out. Evelyn, one of my college dorm mates, and I made plans to drop by Sibley Hospital—located near AU—and then make our way to Tysons Corner, a premier mall in McLean, Virginia. It was picture-perfect day, sunny and not a cloud in the sky. I was driving a sharp-looking teal Mustang that I had borrowed from a male college mate, and Evelyn and I were going shopping at this really cool mall. I remember thinking, Wow, this is going to be a great day! But first—oh, just incidentally—I was going to get this leg checked out.

Although things didn't quite work out as planned, I still took it lightly when an X-ray showed what was described as a growth in my bone.

"Well, no big deal," I told the doctors. "Just take it out."

"It's not that easy," one of them said. "It's a bit more serious than that."

* * *

While the doctors didn't blurt out a diagnosis or mention anything about a "tumor" or "cancer" to me at the time (probably because I was only 17), I did find it curious that they mentioned the skiing prowess of Edward Kennedy Jr. Although I didn't understand why at the time, I would later learn that the famous senator's son had lost a leg to cancer.

A hospital staff member called my mother, and she arrived a little later with her minister. I'm pretty sure the doctors told her they suspected I had cancer, even though the diagnosis could not be confirmed until a biopsy was done. But I believe that she ignored them because their prognostication conflicted with her belief system as a newly converted Pentecostal. I was getting a bit worked up and had by then been given a dose of Librium to calm my nerves, so I was out of it and don't know for sure what they told her.

Regardless, when we left Sibley Hospital that day, my mother, her minister, and I all went into denial, even as my pain persisted.

That's what we humans do, right? Ignore the problem. Ignore the pain. Believe that it will simply go away.

Above anything else in my life, I guess this experience is what really taught me what a powerful force denial can be. At the time, neither I nor any of my family members were willing to hear that type of bad news. I couldn't slow down for something as insignificant as pain. Please. I had way too many plans for my future to allow mere discomfort to slow me down. I was not interested in hearing about such problems—my own or anybody else's.

By then, I had become an expert at ignoring my pain, and I just went on doing the same thing I'd done for months. I just kept on stepping—to classes, to social events, to wherever and whatever. Despite the worsening pain and even the development of a profound limp, I remained active.

By the time my leg finally broke in January 1976, I had probably been walking around on a diseased and painful leg for about a year, hoping that the pain would ultimately just go away on its own somehow. It didn't. Instead, it kept trying to get my attention until it finally succeeded. From October until January, the deadly cancer had continued eating away until my poor leg couldn't take it anymore. I had been moving into my future at warp speed, but something frightening stepped in and said, "Hold up!"

Yes, despite our best efforts, pain will eventually have its say.

5

Between the Devil and the Deep Blue "C"

When I was at NCI in January 1976, after my leg broke, I had a roommate named Curly. She was a young girl from Youngstown, Ohio, with fair skin and the most beautiful long black hair. She quickly became my best friend on Ward 5.

Before I arrived, Curly had already had an amputation—a hip disarticulation, which means her leg was amputated at the hip.

At NCI, I was surrounded night and day by sick children, teenagers, and young adults like me who were all staring death in the face. I was terrified as I lay in my room and observed the small prostheses being carried by nurses down the halls, where cancer was winning the battle over some and leaving others behind to wonder who would be next.

Whenever I was having a bad day or cried, Curly would lie in her bed and say comforting words to me and vice versa. When she had her first day of chemo-therapy, it was terrifying for both of us.

Neither of us talked about death, either because we feared it so much or because we were so consumed with our daily encounters with doctors and nurses poking us and sticking us with needles and such.

Her minister or family members were always in the room praying and offering messages of hope, and my mother, who visited me daily, often read me Bible verses to strengthen my faith.

In mid-February, however, I had to say good-bye to Curly when my mother demanded that I be trans-ferred on a gurney back to our apartment.

* * *

Although my doctors had highly recommended am-putation and chemotherapy treatments to try to stop the cancer from growing and spreading, my mother had her own ideas. She believed that my cancer was the Devil's work, and Pentecostal wisdom direct-ed that all healing be turned over to the power of prayer. My mother was new in the religion, and I believe that she viewed my illness as her first real test of faith.

My three sisters and I had been baptized in the Baptist tradition, and this Pentecostal viewpoint was quite different from what we were used to. The way I understand it, Pentecostals believe that everything in the material world is a symbolic manifestation of the spiritual world. As such, objects, events, and circumstances are either of God or of the Devil. You can guess which side cancer fell on.

My mother believed that my body had been invaded by the Devil himself, and in her opinion, the doctors were part of the Devil's plan because God wouldn't let me lose my leg. As far as she was concerned, my doctors just didn't know what they were talking about. She believed that I didn't even have cancer or need an amputation and that God was going to heal me.

Once I was home, my mother and her Pentecostal brothers and sisters stripped my bedroom of all of the accoutrements of my young life—celebrity posters, pictures, and all other "worldly trappings"—and the prayer vigil was on.

As they worked and prayed, I lay in bed with my diseased leg in a cast—alive but nearly dormant.

My parents had divorced when I was in the sixth grade, but my father lived nearby and was very much a part of my life. Although he didn't share my mother's beliefs and couldn't believe that she was handling my illness this way, he was unable to alter her way of thinking. All he could do was watch with horror as my illness worsened.

■ ■ ■

"Donna, are you all right in there?" my mother asked me through the bedroom door one day.

"Yes, I'm fine," I lied.

I tried to maintain a strong front for others, but when I was alone in my room, it was another story. I often broke down and sobbed uncontrollably. A cancer diagnosis, especially in those days, was almost like a death sentence, and I believe that my fear of imminent death—of extinction—was probably similar to that a prisoner condemned to death must feel in the days and hours leading up to his or her execution. Getting my mind off the cancer was almost impossible, just as it must be for a condemned prisoner alone in a prison cell to get his or her mind off the hangman's noose, the gas chamber, or the firing squad as the clock ticks away toward the inevitable.

Yes, I was scared to death, but because of my nature to try to be strong, I had to deal with the fear largely on my own.

"All right, sweetheart," my mother said. "Good night then."

"Good night, Mom," I said, as I quietly sniffled and wiped the tears from my eyes.

I did not have many people around me because my mother was very protective of me and didn't allow many family members or friends to visit. The spiritual war was on, and she was not going to risk losing the battle to nonbelievers.

I didn't think that anyone else knew or understood what I was going through, and I didn't see how they could relate anyway.

As a result, I felt all alone, comforted only by the lyrics of the Rodgers and Hammerstein song for the musical *Cinderella*, "In My Own Little Corner," which had left an indelible imprint on my mind.

6

Staring Death in the Face

After I had been home for about two weeks and there was no sign the cancer had exited my body, my mother took me for a second opinion at the city's first and only public hospital, DC General Hospital, which closed in May 2001 after serving the city's residents for nearly two hundred years.

This move terrified me.

Although DC General was best known for saving the lives of gunshot victims, somehow my mom believed that if the doctors there could save criminals from gunshot wounds, surely they could save my leg from cancer. Her faith that God was going to save my leg still made it nearly impossible for her to believe that amputation was a solution.

■ ■ ■

"Don't worry, Donna," my friend Vanda would say when she'd visit or call me. "Everything'll be all right." But I could see the doubt in her eyes or hear it in her voice as she spoke.

It was even more difficult for my doctors and nurses to give me the faith to struggle on. They knew the truth, and it was difficult for them to tell me the lie to my face.

"Donna," they'd say, struggling to be positive, "people have beaten this type of cancer before."

Of course, that itself was not a lie. The lie was in what they didn't say. Yes, people had beaten osteogenic sarcoma, but only a very few of them if the disease had already spread when it was first discovered. The survival rate for this type of cancer was and still is very low.

My family—except for my mother, who refused to believe that God would let cancer win—also couldn't erase the fear from their eyes and voices when they sat with me. All of their comforting words were nothing but lies. Yes, well-intentioned lies told with love. But still untrue. They knew it, and I knew it.

7

Taking Control

One evening as my mother sat in the chair next to my hospital bed, she and I discussed the same subject we'd discussed many times: the healing power of God. This time, however, I was ready to take the conversation in a new direction.

"Yes, Mom," I said. "You know that I believe in God and that He can cure me of this cancer, but what if He wants to do it in a different way than we expect? What if He has a different plan for me?"

"Like what?" my mother asked me, with a serious look on her face.

"Maybe He wants to cure me by taking my leg. Maybe the doctors are right. Maybe I should have the amputation."

My mother was silent.

"I know that you and your church friends have my best interest at heart, Mom, but what if you're all wrong? What if I wait too long to have the amputation, and I die because of it?"

The room was silent. She just sat there. Maybe she didn't agree, or maybe she was just considering my opinion. I don't know. It had taken me a lot of energy to build up to this conversation, and I was too exhausted to continue it.

I rolled over and went to sleep.

I felt better now that I had expressed my opinion. I was beginning to understand that this was my life and I had to make my own decisions.

I had been having my own private revival for a while, and while the Pentecostals were praying and looking for a miracle healing, I had begun to accept that getting rid of my diseased leg was the solution God had in store for me. I became ready for Him to take my leg.

Although the Pentecostals had given me a glimpse of God the Healer, and I'm grateful to them for that, I knew that their ways and means were not necessarily my own. I would have to encounter the Great Healer in my own way as I embarked on my own unique journey.

Against my mother's prayers and wishes, and after months of thinking about it night and day, I finally made *my own decision*. In early March 1976, I transferred from DC General back to NCI by ambulance, minus the flashing lights.

Still, I had to force myself to say the words I dreaded saying, and it took all the strength I had inside me to do it.

"Amputate my leg," I told my doctors. "Go ahead and amputate."

■　■　■

I do not want to leave the impression that I was some fearless, junior superheroine, who put her hands on her hips as her cape whipped in the wind and who laughed at the villain cancer. I was scared out of my mind, paralyzed with fear. Still, through a connection with my greatest ally—my Creator—I had begun to tap into the spiritual power that was my birthright, and armed with that power, I began my journey to realizing my potential and aligning myself with all of life's possibilities.

I could not have articulated it in quite that way at the time, but I felt compelled to move, to act, and to take control of my own life and care.

Although my personality was generally one of patience, not defiance, and I typically had no desire to dominate and was fine with others having the reins, this decision was a turning point for me and signaled my moving from being a teenager to a young adult. It was a shift from having to be concerned about what my parents always thought and felt to being liberated and taking control.

■　■　■

Back at NCI, Curly was my roommate again, and she welcomed me with a smile. I could see what her chemotherapy treatments had done to her, and I was horrified at what I thought might soon also become my fate. She was now bald from the treatments, and I feared that I would soon be bald too.

Just like before, our conversations lasted long into the night, until either Curly or I drifted off to sleep and was soon followed by the other.

Fortunately, later on when I started my type of chemotherapy, it did not cause me to lose my hair. In fact, my hair began to grow like long, twisty weeds. As a result, I recall experiencing something like "survivor's guilt" when I didn't lose my hair like Curly had.

8

Losing My Leg—And My Dream

Fortunately, once I made the decision to go forth with the amputation of my leg, the doctors moved quickly. My amputation surgery was scheduled within two days.

Once such a decision is made, waiting is torturous. I couldn't get my mind off the upcoming surgery no matter how hard I tried. And the closer it got, the harder it became.

In those days, it was unusual to see amputees. I don't know if it was because there were fewer of them then or because they stayed at home, but the only amputee I remember seeing before my cancer diagnosis was a young man that we called "One-Legged Steve." Just the mere image of my pant leg flipped under my waistband like his horrified me. I couldn't imagine that future for myself. And yet, I still felt that I had no choice.

If I had been required to wait any longer for the surgery, I might have changed my mind. Perhaps that's one of the reasons the doctors scheduled it so quickly—or perhaps they just wanted to get the cancer out of my body as quickly as possible to increase my chance for survival. Either way, it was good that they did it swiftly.

When the time for the surgery actually came and they wheeled me to the operating area on a gurney, I don't know if my greatest fear was losing my leg or losing myself and coming out of the operating room a different person. Make no mistake about it; I was terrified of both, but I'm not sure which was more terrifying at the time. Just the physical act of having a leg amputated is difficult enough to deal with. Having a leg amputated when your dream is to be an entertainer—a world-renowned dancer—is exponentially worse. Unfortunately, along with losing my leg, I was also losing my dream.

If I were 18 now and my leg required amputation, there would be some chance of pursuing this dream in some way. In 1976, it just wasn't going to happen. And to make it even less likely, the level of my amputation was quite extreme. To ensure the cancer wouldn't spread, my leg was amputated about eight inches below the hip, leaving me with just enough of my leg for my amputation not to be considered a hip-disarticulation but short enough to make my rehabilitation especially difficult. To make matters worse, I was also scheduled for 18 months of chemotherapy treatments.

As difficult and heartrending as it was, *I* had made the decision to let the doctors amputate my leg and to go forward with the chemotherapy. I believed that I had no choice, but now I had to really think about the full impact these decisions would have on my life.

Lying in the hospital room alone, I wondered what I would be able to do with my life now—if, in fact, I survived at all. My prospects did not look promising.

I couldn't talk to Curly because when I returned from surgery and intensive care, I was placed in a private room, and I never saw or heard from her again. Still, I always think about her and where her journey took her. Although we lost touch, I will never forget her.

Now, I had to face the questions on my own.

Would I be able to pursue my dream of being a dancer?

No.

Would I still be a real and complete woman in the eyes of men?

No.

Would I be able to wear my shorts, my lingerie, and my bathing suit, which revealed my shapely legs for the boys to admire?

No.

Looking back, I now realize how shallow some of my concerns were then, but at the time, they were very serious to me. And I was not shown any examples opposing my outlook. Clearly, I was lost!

■　■　■

My dream of being an entertainer—of singing, dancing, and acting—was not merely the passing fantasy of a teenager. It was something deeply rooted in my being.

I had loved singing and dancing as far back as I could remember. As I was growing up, music was everywhere I turned. Our house was filled with the beautiful sounds of such greats as Billie Holiday, Nancy Wilson, Esther Phillips, and Dinah Washington. My mother sang around the house, and so did I. I was a natural; it was in my DNA.

I did not sing in the church choir, but, boy, did I shout out the hymns we sang during the service. I still remember the smiles and approving nods of the church members seated in the front pews at Upper Room Baptist Church. I was able to mimic many sounds and could sing like a variety of singers. Although I mainly sang soprano, I could also sing alto.

When I was around the age of 6, the street corners were where the action was. In the evenings, there'd be boys standing under the streetlamps harmonizing popular tunes.

My sister Margo was three years older than me, and I would tag along with her when she visited her girlfriends who had brothers who sang in groups. Even though Margo could not sing a lick herself, she had several friends who could, and I admired them all.

My neighborhood was full of talented people. Most of my childhood friends could either draw, paint, write, sing, or dance, and many singing groups, including The Unifics and The Intrepids, were born there.

I guess you could say that I was nursed on music, especially if you take into consideration my mother's love for singing and both my parents' love for music. My family always had two things: a working automobile and a hi-fi stereo system. With my parents and my older sister buying records, and my spending my allowance on them from time to time, our home was always full of music. Just like the food we ate to nourish our bodies, music nourished our souls. I still marvel at my mom's record collection, which she still has today.

■ ■ ■

Although my parents could not afford expensive private dance lessons for my sisters and me, we took advantage of all the free dance classes at our local recreational centers. When I was 7, I enrolled in tap, and I really loved the shiny patent-leather shoes with ribbons and the sound they made. Even then I felt like a star.

I also loved *American Bandstand*, *Teenarama*, and *Soul Train*. These TV dance shows helped me hone my dance skills, and then I got a chance to practice them whenever there was a school dance or neighborhood birthday party.

In junior high school, I was a cheerleader and a member of the drill team. When we performed our routines during our schoolwide events, I felt as if everyone was watching me!

Then, when I got a starring role in the school play *Purlie*, my dream was sealed. I knew from the moment I stepped onto that auditorium stage at Carter G. Woodson Junior High School that I was bound for stardom. The applause, the stage lights, and the ovations were intoxicating.

Later, as part of a girls' group, I sang in a talent show, and that was another defining moment. We wore white pants and black-and-white midriff tops, and the audience went crazy when I flawlessly hit the high notes in my solo part of the song "Step Into My World," by The Magic Touch.

Another member of the group—Sharon Graham—and I harmonized well together, and we both were very vain, but on that day, I was the star, and Sharon was my greatest cheerleader. She remains one of my best friends today, and we still sometimes go down memory lane and talk about our moment as stars at that talent show. I sang my heart out that day.

It's funny. Sharon recalls us winning third place. I simply recall us winning.

No, this dream was not a passing fantasy that I could give up easily. It would take something as bad as cancer and the resulting amputation of my leg to violently tear it away from me.

■　■　■

In the hospital, I couldn't get certain negative thoughts and words out of my mind, no matter how hard I tried.

Handicapped. Disabled. Crippled. Flawed. One-Legged Donna.

I thought this was how others would see me now that I'd lost my leg, but it was, in fact, also how I saw myself. And I did not have much empirical evidence to refute my beliefs. The stigma attached to disability status in American society can be so intense and pervasive that it can overshadow other personal characteristics that comprise the individual's self-concept.

We live in a society that is ability oriented, youth oriented, and beauty oriented, and I had been socialized to believe that a woman's beauty was the sum of her body parts, that the clothes she wore dictated how sexy and beautiful she was, and that looking good outweighed intelligence, wisdom, and spirituality. Therefore, naturally, I now thought that my femininity was compromised.

Because so much of who I was at that age depended on my dream of being a performer and my belief that I was attractive, the loss of these two things immediately destroyed my self-esteem. Without these two important aspects of me, who and what was I now? What defined me? Was it cancer and a missing leg? Was I really, in fact, "handicapped, disabled, crippled, and flawed"? I couldn't think of any beautiful words to describe myself anymore. It seemed that my once-wonderful life was over.

■　■　■

When I had first learned that my leg needed to be amputated, I began experiencing some of the so-called Five Stages of Grief—Denial and Isolation, Anger, Bargaining, Depression, and Acceptance—that Elisabeth Kubler-Ross enumerated in her 1969 book *On Death and Dying*. Although we all experience grief in our own ways and may go back and forth through the grieving process or experience the stages in different orders, Kubler-Ross's observations can help us better understand how people generally deal with loss. And just knowing that these feelings will occur and that they are a natural part of grieving can help us better cope with them.

Actually, from the time I first had pain in my knee, I had been in some form of denial, thinking and subconsciously hoping that the problem would somehow just go away. Then, when I learned I had cancer and would need an amputation, I was also in denial for a while. Ultimately, however, I got past the denial, mainly because I wanted to live, and to do so, I had to face the problem. Still, it took me about five months from the time of my diagnosis to reach that point.

I don't recall expressing anger; I think I was more disappointed, sad, and frustrated than angry. Nor do I recall bargaining, unless it was those times when I tried to make deals with God to convince Him to let me keep my leg and live.

Although I was never diagnosed as clinically depressed, I would "feel depressed" often over the coming years when my amputation—or, more often, other people's reactions to it—caused problems in my life.

Acceptance would come along with adjustment to my life as an amputee, but that would take quite a while.

9

Who Is That Girl?

Although there were a lot of thoughts swirling around in my head at this point, in some ways, I felt a sense of relief after the amputation. I was free, at least to some degree. The loss of that leg was at least the first volley in my battle against cancer and pain. In retrospect, it was also the beginning of my reinvention of myself, my extreme makeover, and my new normal, although at the time that fact was muddled in the trauma and fallout following my surgery.

Unfortunately, my doctors were not optimistic about my recovery, and my first of many more chemotherapy treatments began in April, a week before my 19th birthday. In fact, the amputation really turned out to be only the beginning of my recovery from cancer. At that point, I don't think I fully understood everything that would be required to defeat that terrible, life-threatening disease.

I had to stay in the hospital for months after the amputation, and it took a terrible toll on me, both psychologically and physically. Along with the devastating emotional trauma of fear, loneliness, embarrassment, feelings of loss, boredom, and a feeling that this nightmare would never end, I was also dealing with the trauma to my body from the chemotherapy treatments, from lying in bed over a long period of time, and from the physical therapy I had to do.

Following my surgery, my residual limb (the remaining part of my leg) had been put in a cast, and I had been fitted for a temporary artificial leg. Less than five days after my surgery, my doctors had me up and walking on my artificial leg during grueling, daily physical therapy sessions.

■ ■ ■

One day as I held tightly onto the parallel bars and struggled to walk between them, my physical therapist tried to encourage me.

"Come on, Donna. You can do it," she said. "Just a little farther. Just a little bit farther."

I struggled and sweated—and I hated sweating—but I really wanted to walk and knew that I would have to if I wanted out of the hospital.

As I awkwardly inched forward, I could see myself in the mirror next to the parallel bars, even though I tried not to look. It was suddenly quite shocking to see myself like this. The girl looking back at me from the mirror looked like a total stranger, like a survivor of a concentration camp. Anemic, frail, dispirited.

Is that girl really me? I asked myself. I looked far worse than I had expected, and I almost broke down into tears.

I can't go on like this, I thought. I have to do something.

I certainly was not ready to embrace this "new me" yet. No way.

■　■　■

First, I was trained to use a walker. Then, I used crutches for about eight months before I was actually fitted for my first prosthetic leg, after all the swelling was gone and my residual limb was healed.

I found it difficult to walk with my prosthetic leg without falling, and my prosthetist at the time finally realized that I was going to have little control over it because of my short residual limb. He ultimately identified a solution to help prevent me from falling—fitting me with a safety knee that would resist bending. Unfortunately, adding this feature made my limp more pronounced, and it worked against me years later because the resulting muscle atrophy prevented me from using more advanced legs that were designed to provide a more natural gait and minimize limping.

Once I started wearing my prosthesis, I was able to use a cane. I had never really mastered going up and down stairs with crutches, and being able to use a cane was a major step forward.

Although I was highly motivated to learn to walk again, after the hour or so of physical therapy each session, I welcomed being able to return to my room, where I could just lie back down and daydream about getting some semblance of my life back. While I was extremely nervous about leaving the comfort of my hospital room, I wanted to return to home and school.

Being in the hospital for so long, I had begun to settle into a routine, make friends, and establish a new community there. Getting back to real life seemed like such a distant vision, and I had no idea how things were going to work out.

Anyone who has ever been in the hospital for an extended period of time knows how difficult that experience is. In my case, it really began to feel as if it would never end. Fortunately, there were a few things that helped make it bearable.

I had a great nurse named Gloria, who was extremely kind and funny, and she made me feel as if I were the most important patient in the hospital. She always paid attention, heard my cries, recognized my fears, and made me laugh.

I also had a great physical therapist named Marcia, who was both funny and inspirational. I'm sure that I learned to walk with my prosthesis because of her guidance.

10

No More Tears—Enough Is Enough!

While I was in the hospital, I also began concentrating on bolstering myself spiritually, reading every relevant book I could get my hands on—anything spiritual or with the concept of survival in the title or contents: Khalil Gibran, the Bible, Toni Morrison's *Sula*, Maya Angelou's *I Know Why the Caged Bird Sings*, and so on.

Early on, I had been almost exclusively concerned about the physical aspects of losing my leg and the loss of my looks while I should have been more concerned about having a healthy body, spirit, *and* mind. I knew I had to change—to strengthen my mind and spirit—to fight my battle with cancer. I knew I had a lot of work to do because I did not want to accept the death certificate my doctors were writing for me. Moreover, I didn't just want to survive—I wanted to thrive!

I began to replace negative self-talk like "I can't" with "I can," "I won't" with "I will," and "I believe" with "I know." I grew to appreciate silence and self-awareness. Basically, I turned within. My inner self began to grow stronger, and I truly believed that everything was in God's hands.

My mother often assuaged my fears with daily verses from the Bible. One of my favorite and most uplifting passages even today comes from Deuteronomy 31:8 (English Standard Version): "It is the Lord who goes before you. He will be with you; he will not leave you or forsake you. Do not fear or be dismayed." To calm myself, I would often repeat in my mind, "God would not have brought you this far to forsake you."

■ ■ ■

I had such high expectations of myself, and sometimes I just did not feel that I was making great progress. That's how I realized that chemotherapy was not part of my future.

One day, I sat in a chair in my hospital room and watched the chemotherapy drip into the intravenous tubing and then run into my arm like I had so many times before. I had already begun to see the chemotherapy as both medicine and poison—as both friend and foe. The question, however, was where the line separated the two. Was it more a friend, trying desperately to save my life and seeming to have some success, or was it more a foe, poisoning my body and destroying me drop by drop?

I wasn't sure.

I couldn't actually *see* how it was helping against the cancer. I mean, I was still alive, but how could I know that it was the chemotherapy that was making that possible?

On the other hand, I could see how it was affecting the rest of me. And if I had to vote at that moment on whether it was more a friend or foe, I would have had to check the box marked FOE.

That day, as the white-coated staff members moved around me looking at lab results and answering their pagers, I was dealing with a low mood times ten. I grew increasingly impatient with that infamous drip that all chemotherapy patients know. Then came the fatigue, the taste of metal in the back of my throat, and the prolonged weariness of despair and depression.

During my six months of chemotherapy, I regurgitated almost everything I ate, it always left me exhausted, and I dropped from 110 to 85 pounds. I broke down into tears every three and a half weeks when I had to receive another dose. I lost my spirit, and my hope was wavering.

By the sixth treatment, I hit an emotional wall, and I knew that I could not go on.

My life smelled antiseptic and tasted like toxic metals. I could no longer sit compliant with poisonous substances dripping into my veins, feeling sick and as if I were at death's door. I felt that the world was leaving me behind while I languished in some kind of limbo.

I was talking to God and feeling, without a doubt, that He knew me and was ready to guide me. I thought, if it's God's will to have me die, I am going to die outside this hospital well, not sick.

Then one day, when my attending physician came into the room, I was ready to declare my right to really live again.

"Enough," I said. "Unhook me from my chemotherapy. I can't take it anymore."

■　■　■

My decision to stop my chemotherapy was the result of emotional weariness, chemical physical abuse, and psychological trauma. It was an abrupt act. I honestly had no idea that morning that I would redirect my treatment and my life. Some people (probably most) thought I was making a mistake. They believed that the chemotherapy treatments increased my chances of survival. My decision was not based on any type of rational calculation, however; it occurred at the emotional level when my tolerance for the treatment was simply exhausted.

Although I didn't know exactly what was going to happen when I made that decision, I knew that somehow I would be taken care of. I trusted God, and I believed that this trust would just have to carry me through. My doctors thought that I had lost my mind and predicted only a 15 percent chance of survival, but I felt that I had to do what I believed was best for me. This was a huge decision because people in those days rarely questioned a doctor's opinion. I can't really describe strongly enough what it was like to make this decision when my doctors thought it was a death sentence. I didn't know how long I had to live after that.

When I made the decision to come off chemotherapy, against the advice of my doctors and conventional wisdom, it represented my courage to embrace the poetic words *come what may*. I did not want to die, but if it was my time, so be it. It was a paradigm shift in my life. At that moment, I made the decision to live life on my terms. Please note that I am not encouraging other cancer patients to stop their chemotherapy, but being willing to take charge of what is being done to your body is a good rule of thumb for everybody. I had finally proclaimed to the world that it was *my* life and *my* choice.

While my decision represented a further disengagement from my parents and others deciding big issues for me, it was not a conscious effort to do so. It was just a pure emotional reaction, where one just says, "Enough is enough!" So I said, "To hell with it." I spoke to God and left my life or death with Him on the hospital's nightstand. Whatever He decided, I had to live with, but I decided that day that I could not spend another second of my life in the hospital.

The step out of the treatment center that day was equal in magnitude to the step up on the bus that put me in the hospital in the first place. In retrospect, it was the first step of the rest of my life, and while I didn't acknowledge it at the time, it was a definitive moment in my life as a cancer survivor. You don't plan on coming to a fork in the road, and it's not always obvious which direction to take. You just do it!

■　■　■

After that day, each time I returned to the NIH for a checkup and was still cancer-free—for twenty-one years—it was a testament to God's miracles. It reminds me of the words of writer Zora Neale Hurston in *Dust Tracks on a Road*: "I have been in Sorrow's kitchen and licked out all the pots. Then I have stood on the peaky mountain wrapped in rainbows, with a harp and a sword in my hands." Those days and nights I spent at the NIH were indeed often sad and gloomy, but in the end—after the surgery, the physical therapy, and the chemotherapy treatments—I felt victorious and triumphant!

■ ■ ■

When you take chemotherapy, it can affect your senses in strange ways. My sense of smell became dulled, colors appeared flat, my hearing became muted, my vision became myopic, and I couldn't think straight at times. Everything seemed dull, dark, and grayish.

Then when I left the NIH and entered the "normal world," I experienced a sudden sensory overload. Noise was everywhere, people were scrambling, and I had an elevated heart rate and a mild sweat. Red was very red, and the sun seemed extremely bright. My biology and my chemistry were no longer seeking a divorce and were starting to come back together in a new and exciting relationship. My body was in sync with itself again, and the next step was now up to me. My first order of business was to smell the roses because I was still on the right side of the grass—above it!

Life was back on!

"God is the Giver and the Gift."

—FLORENCE SCOVEL SHINN

11

Loss Upon Loss Upon Loss

At home, the fallout from my decision was as expected—chaotic. The consensus was that I had lost my mind—that perhaps the chemotherapy had fogged my thinking—but I proclaimed from that day until now that I had actually finally come to my senses. I had merely found the resolve to act on what I had been wanting to do all along. And now the rhythm of my life could go on without the hated sound of "The Drip."

I understood other people's horror at my choice, but once I had cut through my emotions and evaluated the choices as they really were, I still believed I had made the best decision I could, and I believed that it was correct.

When a person loses one or more limbs, it not only changes him or her physically, but it also has a great emotional impact, especially on the person's self-esteem. He or she might not only feel "less" physically but also "less" as a person. The loss is devastating, and because it is based on a physical loss, there is a constant physical reminder of one's having become "diminished."

Not many people who knew me then or who know me now would accuse me of having low self-esteem by nature, but it wasn't easy for me to accept that I was no longer a whole person physically.

Unfortunately, as difficult as it may be to believe today, in 1976 no one was going to send me to counseling or to any kind of program to help me deal with the emotional trauma that being a teenage cancer survivor and amputee might involve. In those days, the medical model for working with disability was heavily emphasized. The medical model of disability focuses on the individual's limitations and ways to reduce those impairments and use adaptive technology to adapt him or her to society. The social model of disability and the psychosocial aspects of disability, on the other hand, were not part of the conversation. Instead, strategies aimed at helping me live my life as "a cripple"—a term now considered offensive but that was often used for people with disabilities in those days. The focus was on how to navigate the world in a wheelchair, and early on, I had been pressured to adopt the wheelchair as my mode of transportation—something that I strongly rejected. There was a greater stigma to disability at that time, and I had no interest in such a highly visible disability-associated identity. Instead, when I left the hospital after spending a total of about four months there, I had two other pieces of equipment with me: a prosthesis and a set of crutches.

My prosthesis was what was called a test leg, an ugly, mechanical-looking thing with no cover that was sometimes visible under my clothing. Moreover, the prosthesis and my crutches turned my previously sauntering gait into an awkward mess, which I thought destroyed any sex appeal I had left. The possibility of my ever sauntering again was low. Walking with a noticeable limp, a bulge in my clothing, and crutches was my new reality. I hated the way I walked and was embarrassed by it. I couldn't imagine being on stage in a red satin dress ever again. What a nightmare!

While I'd once gotten "good" attention for my performing and from men who found me attractive, I was now getting "bad" attention. Needless to say, this new image did not correspond with my previous view of myself as "Prima Donna." Instead, some people had begun to see and treat me as "Poor Donna" with limited expectations for my future, and often, during bouts of self-pity, I saw myself that way as well.

My immediate family members, on the other hand, weren't ready to allow that type of self-pity.

They expected me to adjust—and to adjust fast. My mother was a single parent, and our family lived in a third-floor apartment, so I had to find a way to at least get up and down stairs and navigate my environment. If I wanted to survive outside the hospital, I had to learn to adjust physically even if I still had not adjusted emotionally.

From right after my amputation, I had started defining "normalcy" as "walking without a limp." I could never imagine leaving the house without my artificial leg.

Society was at that time, and still is today, very much concerned with the way a person looks, and I knew that I wanted to look good after my amputation. That's one of the ways I tried to counter some of the negative views of me.

Since my prosthesis made my clothing look awkward, and my limp was too extreme to hide, I really had to put forth a lot of extra effort to look the way I wanted to. Still, I made it a priority, regardless of the cost.

■ ■ ■

"I am *not* going to wear Hush Puppies," I told myself one day, laughing while trying to keep from crying. Although Hush Puppies were the footwear prescription of choice for people with amputations in those days, I rebelled against them. In the '70s, platform shoes were popular, and I couldn't believe that the rehabilitation folks expected me to leave my platforms and go down to Hush Puppies! Please. The thought alone was traumatizing enough.

There was just no way that was going to happen! I'm not downing Hush Puppies, but I was definitely a heels type of gal.

This was one area of my life where I had to put my foot down. I guess I somehow knew that the footwear and clothes I chose—my style of dress—would affect my identity in important ways.

I still wanted to be a princess, a diva, a star—and princesses, divas, and stars did not wear Hush Puppies. They were definitely not part of the identity I was going for.

Of course, my looks were not going to define my whole new life, but they were a piece of it—an important piece to me.

Although walking with a noticeable limp is my reality, I found a great cobbler who could fix my shoes so that the heel heights were just right to lessen my limp. Also, since I couldn't fathom wearing a dress over the prosthesis with the way it caused humps and bumps, I wore pants. In fact, I would not wear a dress again until about ten years after my amputation.

Everything about us helps create our persona, and we can plan the persona we want and then do things— like wearing certain clothes, driving a certain type of car, living a certain way, getting a certain education or job, and so on—to help us develop that persona and become that type of person.

I'm not saying that clothes, cars, houses, and cell phones can make the person. I mean, you can't put a crown on and suddenly become a princess or prince. At the same time, these things do affect our identity in some profound ways. How we dress, the car we drive, and the phone we have do make others see us in a certain way. And they also affect how we see ourselves and feel about ourselves.

If someone, for example, drives up in an old truck and wearing jeans, cowboy boots, and a cowboy hat, we will likely assume that person is a cowboy or cowgirl or a country music singer. If the same person drives up in a Mercedes and wearing an expensive business suit, we will probably assume that he or she is a businessperson, salesperson, doctor, lawyer, or some other professional. Also, that person, depending on how he or she shows up and is dressed, might also begin to feel like and identify with that assumed persona.

In my case, had I followed the Hush Puppies prescription and worn such casual shoes and then dressed in the way that went with them, I would have been seen as more practical and less flashy and attractive. That is not what I wanted. I wanted—even with my missing leg, prosthesis, and limp—to be seen as fashionable, attractive, sharp, and sexy. To do so, I needed to dress the part. Fortunately—or unfortunately, depending on how we deal with them—these things can start to become self-fulfilling prophecies.

■ ■ ■

Unfortunately, no matter how well I dressed, people still stared when they saw me limping along. It was obvious to them that something wasn't quite right, but what? The word *uncomfortable* doesn't even begin to describe what I was feeling. I was devastated.

Even though I had always been an attention seeker, this was the wrong kind of attention, and I no longer wanted to be in the spotlight. Who—especially a teenager—wants to get so much negative attention? At the time, I didn't want to stand out; I wanted to fit in. At a minimum, I might have even accepted being unnoticed or invisible.

But that was not to be.

■ ■ ■

"Hello," I said excitedly as I picked up the phone on the third ring and held it to my ear.

"Hey, Donna," my friend Celeste said. "Belinda and I are planning to hit the club tonight. Are you in for going out with us and maybe also catching a movie or getting something to eat?"

"A girls' night out! Yep. Count me in," I said, excited about the opportunity to get out of the apartment. I'd been pretty grounded since my amputation months earlier, and I'd finally learned to get up and down the stairs to our apartment without killing myself.

"OK. I'll blow the horn when we arrive in front of your building," Celeste said.

"Great! I'll be ready."

I recall the excitement of that day as if it were yesterday. I hurriedly got dressed, and by about 6:45, I was ready to party with my friends. I grabbed my stylish cane and headed out the door.

"Have fun," my mother said, "and be careful!"

I laughed and started down the steps, taking my time, making sure not to trip or miss a step.

I was waiting out front when my friends arrived a little early.

"Wow," Belinda said. "Don't you look cute?"

I smiled and accepted the compliment.

"Thanks," I replied confidently. "This is the first time I've been out of the house for the last few days, and I want to be sure I leave a lasting impression on everyone."

We changed our plans and headed in the direction of Landover Mall, a premier shopping destination in the late '70s. At that time, the mall included Sears, Garfinckel's, Woodward & Lothrop (Woodies), Hecht's, and a six-screen theater. It was always fun to go there to shop and people watch.

We found a place to park, got out of the car, and started walking toward Woodies' main entrance.

"Wow, check out that hot guy over there to our left," Celeste said.

"Oh yeah!" I agreed. "Sizzlin'!"

We continued on, laughing and joking, pointing out other good-looking guys and acting silly like we always did when we got together. It was just like old times.

Then, in the midst of our fun—and seemingly out of nowhere—rain started coming down in torrents. Celeste and Belinda shrieked and then covered their hair and start running toward the nearest shelter before they got too wet.

Unfortunately, unlike my friends, I couldn't run. All I could do was try to cover my head and start limping along toward the nearest store's entrance. The parking lot was slick now, and suddenly my prosthetic leg went one way and my real leg another. I fell fast and hard. My pants were wet; my hands and knees were scraped; and I'm pretty sure that my lipstick was smeared. I wanted to cry.

Extremely embarrassed, I looked around quickly to make sure that not too many people had seen me, especially any guys, and then I struggled to my feet. I was soaked, my hair was messed up, and my clothes were dirty. Still, as bad as that was, my pride was hurt even more.

Dammit! I thought. Dammit!

This type of scene would happen more than once. When I went out with my friends, I often couldn't keep up, and if it would start to rain, they would run ahead for shelter while I had to limp slowly along. When there was snow or ice, I'd either risk falling or have to depend on someone else to help me.

Although I never cried in front of others, I would often break down in tears later, when I was alone and able to reflect on my hidden emotions. Learning to walk on my artificial leg was daunting, and as hard as I tried, I couldn't get rid of the limp or the possibility of falling down in public.

■ ■ ■

Since I knew that I needed to "do something with my life," I finally decided to go ahead with my plans to pursue my education. By fall of 1977, just a year after my amputation, I was back in school at American University and doing my best to fit in with all the other students.

Then one cold, rainy day on campus, I was navigating slowly toward my class to keep from falling. As I got near the steps leading up to the building where my class was held, I sensed two students coming up behind me.

They probably didn't think I heard them when the young man whispered to the young woman, "Hurry and get past that crippled girl before we get to the steps, or we'll be late for class."

As the students blew past me, I stepped to the side and hoped that no one else had heard the hurtful words the young man had said.

Embarrassed, I waited to make sure that no one was behind me before I started limping up the steps.

The words *crippled girl* went through my mind with every step I took.

After that day, I would always try to wait until no one else was around before starting up or down steps because I didn't want to hear other students sigh or rush to get past "the crippled girl." Even though I would have to arrive extra early to class and be the last one to leave, it was worth it to spare myself the humiliation I felt that day.

■　■　■

Wherever I went, whatever I did, I was constantly reminded about my disability. Everyone seemed to want my missing leg to mean that I was some kind of pitiful or damaged object—someone that either had to be fixed or shunned.

As I walked toward some people, they would scurry away. I often wondered if they perhaps thought I had something contagious or that my disability might somehow rub off on them. And I don't even know how many times I heard someone say, "Kids, get out of that girl's way; she's handicapped."

Other people, including complete strangers, would interrupt me and ask what was *wrong* with me.

"What do you mean what's *wrong* with me?" I often wanted to yell.

It always shocked me when I was minding my own business and someone would come from out the blue and ask me this question. It made me very uncomfortable, especially when it came from a man. I would tense up immediately because I knew that he would not be prepared for my answer. And I was also not prepared for his reaction.

I often wanted to say, "Why do you care that I walk with a limp? Why do you ask me what happened to my leg before you even ask me my name? Did I speak to you? No, so why are you asking what happened to me as if we know each other?"

"Did you break your leg?" they would ask. "Did you have a hip replacement? Did you sprain your ankle?"

"No. No. No. I just have one leg; I am an amputee. I lost my leg to bone cancer."

"No way!" they'd say. "You are much too attractive to be walking like that. In fact, why do you walk like that when some people have bionic legs? When you buy shoes, do you buy one shoe or a pair? Are you freaky in bed? Is sex with you a blast? I've heard some stories about chicks like you. Can you have babies?"

I was constantly worried about how I appeared to others. Every person I encountered was a potential commentator or critic. That could add up to dozens of potential critics every day.

I especially remember hating it when full-service gas stations changed to self-service because it meant that I had to get out of my car and pump my own gas. I could no longer sit inside and hide behind the steering wheel. The safe places—the places I could hide from other people's stares and questions—were quickly disappearing.

■　■　■

After my amputation, I already felt that my body was "deformed," and I didn't think I was sexy looking anymore. Nobody had to tell me this. I felt it on my own.

I was also discovering that my amputated leg was an issue for men I found attractive, including those I was already involved with.

When I first lost my leg, my steady boyfriend did not forsake me because of my amputation, but he did not assure me that he loved me in spite of it either. In fact, when I unexpectedly showed up at a party he was at one night after my amputation, he seemed to be ashamed of me.

The "missing leg thing" and the limp just seemed to be something guys couldn't handle.

Problems I encountered in a relationship with another man I dated before and after my amputation were also a profound blow to my self-image and self-esteem. The second part of the relationship, which occurred after my amputation, ended abruptly because my man could not rewire his brain and process that a woman could still be complete with one leg. Although he seemed to be able to deal with my new body as long as I was wearing my artificial leg, he was unable to deal with it once I removed the artificial leg and he saw my residual limb. It seemed that he could only perceive me as the sum of my body parts. Since I had less than what is considered the normal number of parts, he saw me as less than a full woman. This, of course, did not help me feel "normal" and, in fact, made me feel unworthy of a man's desire.

To overcome my self-doubt and insecurities about my fullness as a woman and to regain my confidence and belief that I was worthy, I became overly sexualized and promiscuous. I was ashamed of my amputated leg and was not convinced that any man would find me sexy, so I began to lower my standards to make having sex with me easy. I quickly consented to sex with men on first dates, even though such behavior was in direct opposition to my spiritual values. By doing so, I essentially murdered and buried my self-esteem.

Since I did not value myself, and therefore no one else could value me, I found myself going through a revolving door of one-night stands, trying to get the approval I was seeking. I wanted—and needed—to be desired at any cost. As a result, I continued to make poor choices for boyfriends, and although I was never physically abused, I did experience emotional abuse.

My self-doubt and self-pity grew even worse as I continued to find no answers to the questions I had: Why me? Why cancer? Why my leg? Why now?

I believed that no one could imagine what I was going through. I had been stripped of so many things that many people take for granted: the ability to take a simple walk to class, to run through a park, to play a sport, or to pursue my dreams. The ability to be loved totally and unconditionally.

I couldn't help feeling like society's outcast.

12

The Whole World Is a Stage

At some point, this new perception of myself—a person with no value because I'd lost a leg—would either destroy me or have to be challenged.

In the midst of all this difficulty, I also had some good things going for me. Although I felt like giving up many times, I realized that I didn't have a gene for quitting. I had always been an achiever, someone who was motivated and who believed she was destined for greatness. I also knew that I couldn't give up because others were looking to me to teach them. I didn't want my family, my friends, and others to see me fall down. So each time I stepped out of my door, I had a purpose—to show that I could still succeed.

■ ■ ■

Although I lost sight of it from time to time, I think I inherently knew that my strength lay in a deep place within me that no one could see. Down deep, I knew that my body parts were in service to this God-given soul, not the other way around.

I decided that it was now time to think about how to upgrade myself from "Poor Donna"—the way I was now perceived by many—to something else.

My decision to return to school was probably the most important decision I made after my amputation and quitting chemotherapy. Had I not returned to school to earn my bachelor's degree, my entire life would probably be different. Had I stopped my education, my possibilities would have been so much more limited, and I very well could have had a life of victimhood and hopelessness. Getting my bachelor's degree was the first step on the path to who and what I would ultimately become. Instead of using my disability as an excuse to do nothing, I quickly jumped back into life.

I had a new plan for that life, and I began to pursue it without delay. Instead of being a world-renowned performer, singing and dancing at the Apollo or Carnegie Hall before thousands of adoring fans, I would be a different kind of performer on a different kind of stage. My new stage would be the classroom, and my new audience would be my students. I would be a teacher.

I focused on getting my degree in elementary and early childhood education. This change represented a deconstruction of my old self in order to reconstruct a new self. I had to first accept that I was an amputee and come to grips with the fact that I was not going to be able to live my life as I had for the past 18 years. In essence, I had to reorganize my thoughts so that I would be able to have the strength to live and thrive with my disability. Because I knew that I did not want to live my life always bemoaning the fact that my leg was amputated, I decided that I must revel in the blessing with which I had been bestowed. I had to understand that the fact that I survived cancer was much greater than the loss of a limb—or a dream.

13

Running Away

Even though it was a struggle to get around the campus at American University, I worked hard and graduated in the spring of 1979 with a bachelor's degree.

Not long afterward, in September of that year, I landed my first teaching job at a Catholic school, Our Lady Queen of Peace, teaching second graders. No longer relying on financial aid, and with my own apartment and car, I was basking in my freedom and financial independence.

Still, being in DC, I would often encounter someone who'd known me before my amputation or who had heard about my amputation "through the grapevine." Yeah, the DC grapevine was busy, and as usual, it was disseminating a lot of erroneous information.

"Have you heard the news about Donna Walton? She had both her legs amputated and is in a wheelchair now."

"Remember Donna Walton? She's bedridden now—paralyzed from the neck down. Doctors say she'll never walk again."
"Poor thing."

"Did you hear about Donna?"
"No, what?"
"She got cancer and died!"
"No! I can't believe it. She was such a sweet girl."

"They buried Donna Walton last week. The service was beautiful, I heard."

OK. I'm partly joking and partly serious. The things I heard from others about what happened to me were sometimes totally wrong, and I would have to go through the difficulty of reliving the details of my cancer, chemotherapy, amputation, and life with a disability to correct the rumors.

I was being constantly reminded of what I had gone through and that I was different. As a result, I decided that I needed a big change of some kind in my life. Perhaps I could avoid many of these experiences, I thought, if I moved to another city—somewhere far away. I was now ready to create my own recipe for living the life I desired, but to do so, I needed to get away from DC so that I could start over.

In the summer of 1980, I began to devise a plan.

■　■　■

"Why Texas?" asked Maya, one of my best friends since junior high school, when I told her about my plan to move to Houston. "I thought you always wanted to move to LA to pursue your dream of becoming an actress. I thought we were going to go there together. Why in the world would you want to move to Texas?"

She was screaming now, unable to understand my unexpected decision.

As I tried to compose some kind of answer that would satisfy her curiosity and calm her down, I stumbled over my words. I ended up saying that I wanted to pursue my teaching career and that there were a lot of well-paying jobs in Houston. At the time, I was only earning $8,000 per year, and I wanted a higher salary, like some of my friends who were earning a whopping $2,000 more than I was at their teaching jobs in public schools.

But this was not the only reason, so I dodged Maya's question. I really just wanted to leave DC. I needed to be able to live away from others' peering eyes, judgment, and pity. I wanted to live out loud, so to speak, where no one was watching me. I wanted to get used to falling, limping, and adjusting to my new look and life away from those who remembered me as I was before my amputation. I figured that strangers would be less vested in me.

Moving away from DC was a great decision for both of us, but we had reached our decisions for different reasons. I *needed* to leave. There was simply no way that I was going to be able to live my own life out loud, on my own terms, and without pity and judgment at home. Still, I also needed to be someplace where there was a semblance of family so that I could find comfort in knowing that I was not truly alone in the Lone Star State. Fortunately, a friend of the family had relocated his family to Houston in 1979. Perfect timing for me.

I changed the subject with Maya.

"Where are you going to live in LA?" I asked. "Who are you going to stay with?" Little did she know that I was profoundly jealous that she was going to move to the place that I had always thought my own dreams would come true.

Another reason I needed to go to Houston instead of to Los Angeles with Maya was my fear that my cancer would return. I had not told Maya that I had terminated my chemotherapy treatments after only six treatments, thereby foregoing the remaining thirteen treatments that had been prescribed. I was not ready to pursue my dreams because I was preoccupied with the fear of the cancer returning each time I would return to the NIH for my six-month checkup.

Even though this conversation took place decades ago, I still sometimes regret my decision not to go to LA with Maya. I sometimes wonder what might have been if I had been a little bolder.

■　■　■

"I found a job in Houston, Texas," I told my mother excitedly as I walked into the kitchen.

"What?" she said. "You never mentioned anything about this before."

"I found a job in Texas, and I'm planning to move there at the end of the school year," I said. "It's a great opportunity for me."

My mother was shocked, but she knew me and how determined I could be, and she didn't argue.

I'd just told my mother a major lie. I had no job in Houston. I just knew that I had to get out of town.

It was one of my earliest attempts to reinvent myself after my amputation, and I knew that I couldn't do it around those who knew me and knew about my amputation and considered me "Poor Donna." I had already heard "Poor Donna" so many times that it could have defined me and led me to a persona of perpetual victimhood if I had allowed it to.

"Poor Donna, but you're still pretty."

"Poor Donna, but…"

So much of who I was had become tied up in how I looked and my disability. Although I didn't know yet exactly how I wanted to redefine myself, I already knew that I didn't want to be seen as "Poor Donna" anymore.

I needed to get beyond that, and I needed to do it without my family and friends watching me.

Although I didn't really have a job in Houston, I was confident that I could find one once I arrived. I had my bachelor's degree and a little professional experience, and I knew that I was good at teaching even though I was just beginning.

14

"You'd Be Perfect!"

"We have an opening to teach special education," the principal of a school in Houston told me during my interview. "You'd be perfect for it."

Although my major was elementary and early childhood education—*not special education*—when he offered me the job, I was happy to be hired to teach severely emotionally disturbed children and felt that it was an honor. I was highly committed to teaching, and being hired as a special education teacher for mostly black children didn't concern me…until later, when I began to think more about it.

For a while, I believed that it was where I needed to be, and I started to get comfortable with it. I started to think that it was good that I had such an opportunity to be around people with disabilities like me.

My life in Houston—a city of pickup trucks, cowboy hats, and humidity—turned out to be

adventurous, quite interesting, and extremely revealing. My self-concept came alive there. It was wonderful to be in a new city and not know anyone except
my one friend. I didn't have to do anything except
show up. It was great not to have to explain my life
to everyone anymore.

And, to a large degree, it worked out! My new ac-
quaintances encountered me on my own terms, and
not being constantly watched and questioned allowed
me to soar.

There were still some times, however, when I was
reminded of my amputation.

When I first moved to Houston, my only experience with a man being really into me was my relationship with my boyfriend who I'd been with from when
I was 15 to my junior year in college.

Now that I was alone and on my own in Houston,
the attention I started getting from men was amazing.
They were like, "Hey, baby. You look good. How can
I meet you?"

Often, as I drove to work in my sporty Subaru, I
noticed guys driving up beside me to check me out. It
seemed that cute men were everywhere on Interstate
10, and lots of them seemed to find me attractive.
In fact, as they raced up beside me and turned their
heads to stare, I'm surprised some of them didn't end
up crashing their cars.

Still, developing any kind of romantic relationship was tough. As long as men saw only my face, arms, hands, and torso, I got plenty of attention. Unfortunately, for some reason or another, I'd ultimately have to get out of my car—maybe to pump my gas or go into a store—and then they'd see my cane and notice my limp.

With many guys, that was fine at first because they'd just assume that my cane and limp were due to something temporary, like a sprained ankle or broken leg.

Amputation, however, was a different matter entirely. Just like in DC, most guys just couldn't handle it. As long as I could hide the amputation, things were fine. But then the dreaded questions would always come up: "What happened to you? What's *wrong* with you?"

So much for the potential for romance. Nothing new there.

15

The Dating Game

The idea of love at first sight has been a fantasy of mine since I was a little girl. The mere thought of my prince whisking me off into the sunset dazzled my thinking about love and marriage. Unfortunately, after amputation, this dream was seemingly a distant blur. Having a man see me and fall in love at first sight eluded me for years after my amputation.

You see, by nature, men are visual creatures. Most men get turned on by the parts of women they can see, not the parts of women they cannot see—such as a missing limb. Even though I seldom enter the world without wearing my artificial leg, when most men encounter me, they notice my appearance—and also my cane that I use to help me walk. This usually leads to rejection, and although this is not a good feeling to anyone, it carries even more weight when you are a woman with a disability.

Long before online dating, there was the concept of blind dating, in which someone you know arranges a date for you with someone you have never seen in person. It is, therefore, the responsibility of the person who arranges the date to ensure that the two are a good match. Sometimes one person is more interested in the match than the other, which may make it more difficult for the matchmaker to judge whether the date will be successful.

I did not care for blind dating much because I always felt like I was being bet on. And during the blind date itself, I always dreaded even more the moment when I would have to answer the dreaded question "What happened to you?" or "Why are you walking like that?"

Neither my intellect nor my looks seemed to be enough to hold a man's attention during a blind date until I was set up on one when I was in Houston.

Richard was a friend of James and Cheryl Craighead, a couple I knew from work. Cheryl told me that they had a really nice friend they called "Cupcake."

I was like, "Cupcake? What a name!"

But Richard sounded adorable, so I agreed to meet him. He was from Pittsburgh and, like lots of people in those days, had moved to Houston for economic reasons. The city was booming because of the oil industry, and there were lots of great opportunities. Richard also agreed to meet me even though he was worried about going on a blind date and was afraid I was going to be a monster.

When he showed up at my door, however, he said that he was amazed.

"You are fine!" he said. He also said that my having one leg was not an issue—that I exceeded all the expectations that he would ever have.

"You're so beautiful that I don't even think about your missing leg," he explained.

He became in awe of me and really admired my intelligence. We dated for a while but ultimately became great friends.

Following is an adapted version of how Richard describes our blind date and subsequent relationship:

Jimmy (Cheryl's husband) said I should meet Donna but would not share anything else about her except that she had a great spirit and personality. In my mind, "a great personality" meant she was ugly. But because my interest was piqued, I asked for her phone number so I could call her and quickly end the Craigheads' attempt at a love connection!

I called her, and our first call lasted for several hours! Now I had to meet her. I called her to see if we could get together, and she agreed, with the proviso that our initial meeting would have to be at her apartment. We lived about fifteen minutes apart, and she gave me her address and directions and said her Subaru was parked right outside her apartment.

I arrived at her place, and as I walked up the steps to her apartment, I braced myself for a lady with a great personality (but surely ugly). How shallow I was then!

Donna opened her door, and there to greet me was a gorgeous woman with a smile for the ages! I remember looking to the heavens and thinking, Thank you, God, and the Craigheads.

As Donna let me in and led the way, I noticed that she was limping, but I just figured that she'd been in an accident and her leg was in a cast.

We talked for hours, and I had never met a woman so well versed on such a myriad of subjects. I know I probably stared at her, admiring how pretty she was. We had clicked, and then Donna declared that before our relationship progressed, she had to clear the air. She told me that she was a cancer survivor, but to save her life, they had amputated her leg above her knee!

Now I knew why the Craigheads withheld this tidbit of information. With my preconceived notions of people with disabilities, I would have never wanted to date her. But I remember thinking how lucky I was to find such a brilliant woman.

Over the months that followed, we became an item. We would go out to dinner, and I knew I was the luckiest guy in town! I discovered that she did not have any disabilities, and it wasn't long before she had me acting like a little kid every time we were together.

After a while, she became comfortable around me and would remove her leg, and I remember thinking what great balance she had.

Well, sadly our love affair fizzled out, and she moved away. Still, there was rarely a day that I did not wonder how life was treating her.

■　■　■

"Do you know how beautiful you are? I think not, my dear. Yet I could set you upon a stage and worship you forever!"

—Hafiz

16

Ease On Down the Road

While I had some negative experiences in Houston, overall it was good for me in many ways. I did some things there that I wouldn't have done in DC. I also began to explore my body concept more deeply and to show my prosthesis a little more. Mainly, though, I had the great opportunity to be on a "stage" (my classroom) with an "audience" (my students).

■ ■ ■

Why would you quit? I asked myself after a period of reflection on my job in Houston. The school system wants you to stay. You're good at your job. The pay is OK. Why quit?

Like many people—probably most—who are considering leaving a job or the place they currently are in their life, I was struggling within, trying to determine if I was doing the right thing.

Although I liked my job and considered it important, for some reason, I felt that it was no longer right for me. The job of teaching children with disabilities had not been my original goal and had been placed upon me by a school system that seemed to believe that since I had a disability, I would be "perfect" for that job.

Over time, however, I began to realize that the school system had directed me toward special education for the wrong reason. I realized that those in charge of the hiring had simply seen me as a person with a disability and thought that this somehow made me qualified to be (or *only* qualified to be) a special education teacher. In the end, I realized that this wasn't the identity I was going for. Something about it just didn't sit right with me anymore.

I realized that it was simply another form of bias—the kind where one is not quite sure what is motivating it. In fact, even later, it seemed that whenever I applied for an elementary school teaching job, I'd always be tagged to teach special education. And that told me something. Therefore, in June 1981, after nearly a year of living and working in Houston, I decided that it was time to move on.

I wanted something else and was willing to take a risk and try something new. Fortunately, we live in a time and in a culture where we can try new things and are not as constrained in our choices as people once were.

■　■　■

That's the truth, but not the whole truth. The whole truth was that there was also a man involved. My friend Celeste had called me a few months earlier and said that she knew a guy I should meet who lived in Syracuse.

Who lives in Syracuse? I thought.

Anyway, I had agreed to talk to him. His name was Noah, and he had started calling me. He was very smart and older. I believe he was 30, and I was 24. It was really nice talking to him, and ultimately, I became enamored with him.

He acted as if he didn't know about my amputation, although my friends had already told him about it.

Eventually we met in person when he flew to Houston from Syracuse.

We developed an exciting relationship, and I fell in love with him and decided that I wanted to be in Syracuse with him. I wasn't sure what I could do there, but then I found out that Syracuse University and the S.I. Newhouse School of Public Communications, one of the best schools in the United States for radio and TV broadcast journalism, were there. I thought, OK, maybe I can give my communications dream a try.

I read a theory that everyone is six or fewer steps away, by way of introduction, from any other person in the world. I started checking out programs, and it turned out that some of my friends had friends who were friends with someone who headed a work-study program in the College of Arts and Sciences at Syracuse University. Talk about six degrees of separation! I decided to apply, and when I received a scholarship and was accepted, I began to believe that it was meant to be.

I moved to Syracuse, got my own apartment, and paid my way with my scholarship and by participating in a work-study program. I was also near Noah.

It was perfect.

For a while.

17

Black, Female, *and* Disabled

Don't Put Me in a Box

Do not try to constrain me.
Never try to fit me in a box
Of your own making.
For I am more—
So much more—
Than you can imagine.
So much more
Than you can force
To fit a tiny space
Limited by your
Lack of vision.

—Donna R. Walton

I was never one to be put in a box.

My vision of my future was always larger, I guess, than the one anyone else had for me.

My mother always said that I was an "ambitious soul."

That was clear when, after my year in Houston, I made the bold decision to move to Syracuse to pursue my master's degree in adult education with the intention of later applying to the S.I. Newhouse School of Public Communications to major in broadcast journalism.

While attending Syracuse University, I also worked as a special education teacher (yes, again) at Blodgett Middle School. I worked there from September 1981 through June 1983, resigning only when I completed all my coursework toward my degree and returned home to DC. At that time, I only needed to complete my comprehensive exams.

While I was pursuing my coursework in education, however, the desire for performing continued to burn within me. Unfortunately, although I was always trying to be a part of performing in some fashion, there were no role models to show me the way. I therefore sought out opportunities wherever I believed I could fit in as a performer, even if they weren't what many would consider "performing."

I had taken some basic courses in TV and radio broadcasting as electives, and they had whet my appetite for broadcasting. My speaking voice was strong, and I had a good command of the English language and could write fairly well, so I successfully found volunteering opportunities at radio stations despite having a degree in education. Earlier, when I was in Houston, I had also secured a volunteer position at an AM radio station.

Now, before completing my master's degree, I acquired a volunteer position at the well-known WOL radio station (known today as Radio One) in DC. Radio One was started by Cathy Hughes, who became the first black American woman in history to head a publicly traded business. Seeing this young black woman as the head of such a formidable radio station was a great inspiration to me, and I thought I wanted to be like her.

Before that, while in Syracuse, I had tried desperately to change my major to communications. One day, I finally built up the courage to meet with the head of the department at the prestigious S.I. Newhouse School of Public Communications and express my passion and profound interest in broadcasting. Unfortunately, my self-worth seemed to deflate right before my eyes when he told me that my SAT scores were not high enough to gain acceptance.

Although I strove to convince him that my test scores were not necessarily a predictor of my ability to succeed, he continued to scoff at my scores and lecture me on the types of students who matriculated there. Feeling like an award-winning actress who was given a terrible review after a stellar performance on stage or a fighter after losing a championship bout, I left his office wilted and stunned.

I am not immune to disappointment, but I fight very hard not to internalize "failure"—not to merely accept it. As a result, I turned that department head's condemning recitation into my greatest motivation to keep trying. The day I was banished from that department head's office, I wanted to succeed even more—to show him and everybody else what I was capable of.

Fortunately, Cathy Hughes at WOL believed in me enough to place me on the air without any formal experience in radio broadcasting. She restored a sense of confidence in me that Syracuse's department head had tried to annihilate. When I was off the air, she called me into her office and said, "Walton, you did a good job," despite my mispronunciation of the last name of Bobby Beathard, former general manager of the Washington Redskins.

■ ■ ■

Later, I prepared myself to try another route to a career in broadcasting. I had heard about a broadcasting internship at a local TV station in Washington, DC, and decided to interview for it. I wanted the position badly and felt that I had all of the qualifications. I was ready to go for it.

When I entered the interviewer's huge office, he was sitting behind a rather small, typical-looking newsroom desk, which made the room appear even larger. Even though he was dressed casually, he was quite intimidating since he was the person who could grant or deny me the internship. He had a grin that made it hard to tell if he was cordial or arrogant, and even though I was trembling inside, I smiled and tried to appear calm.

He had seen me walk in with a limp and a cane, and after I sat down, his first question was about my leg.

"Did you break your leg?" he asked.

"No," I said nervously. "I'm an amputee as a result of cancer."

"Oh," he said. "Oh."

After a brief period of small talk, he got right to "the point," and it seemed that "the point" was not to tell me more about the internship and convince me to take it but rather to find a way to disqualify me.

"So," he said stoically, "what would you do if you were covering a story and had to run to get to it? Wouldn't your prosthetic leg make it impossible for you to get there quickly? Remember we are competing against other stations to get the story first."

"I would find a way to get it, whatever it takes, even if I have to ask the cameraman for assistance," I said, desperately trying to salvage the interview.

Unfortunately, I somehow knew from the look on his face that my answer hadn't satisfied him.

I suddenly felt a lump growing in my throat and a vacuum in my stomach.

No, I didn't get the internship, but I got the message. I think I can say with 100 percent certainty that my disability destroyed any chance I had of getting that internship.

It was the summer of 1984, and despite affirmative-action policies, being black and a woman already counted as two strikes against me when I was seeking employment and other opportunities. Now it seemed that if those two strikes didn't put me out of the game, the third strike—a physical disability—would.

After I left the television station that day, I broke down inside my car and cried. I was really worried about my future. Being black, female, *and* disabled was certainly not a recipe for success in 1984. Each of these three things alone could hinder a person's efforts toward success, but all three combined, it seemed, would make it nearly impossible.

I'll never forget that interview. I knew then that my disability would always be a potentially serious obstacle to my success—that many people simply could not see through my disability to the real me and what I had to offer. As a result, I knew that, for the rest of my life, I would have to strive to become impervious to and rise above the limitations imposed on me by others.

Discrimination can be "in your face" or below the surface, but in the cases where I believed I was highly qualified and sometimes overqualified and was denied an opportunity, it is difficult to believe that my race, gender, and/or disability did not enter into the equation.

These two experiences—my "failure" to be accepted in the broadcasting program at Syracuse and to get the TV broadcasting internship—were, in retrospect, my "Michael Jordan moments."

You might recall hearing Jordan, who is considered one of the best basketball players ever, tell how he missed more than nine thousand shots and missed the game-winning shot in twenty-six games. Still, he said, his many "failures" led to his great success.

Like Jordan, I refused to accept "failure," although that refusal might have been subconscious at the time.

Back then, I was not equipped to critically examine the intersectionality of race, gender, and disability on my survival in the workforce and society's lack of comfort with my "disability look." Had I been more keenly tuned in, perhaps I may have recalled Sojourner Truth, a black woman who made major contributions to the struggles for abolition and women's rights. Although history recalls Truth as a strong black woman with a strong working arm, writer Meredith Minister notes that she, in fact, had a disabled hand, which she sometimes hid or directed attention away from to put forth the idea that women and blacks were able. Just as Truth established her status as a strong black woman with her famous question, "Ain't I a woman?" so too have I come to refuse to accept that I am *only* a black woman with one leg.

Shortly after my "Michael Jordan moments," I completed my master's degree in adult education with combined coursework and internships in broadcasting. While my efforts toward a broadcasting career went to the background as I pursued other goals over the coming years, the idea never left my mind completely.

In retrospect, I can see that nobody was going to put me in a box of his or her making. I was not going to take no for an answer. It was not in my nature. I just wasn't born that way.

18

Growing Up in Turbulent Times

I was born on April 24, 1957, in Washington, DC. At the time, the nation was divided by race, and I was on the side with the least opportunity. Although the greatest divisions were in the Deep South, the city of my birth, the nation's capital, was not immune. Dwight D. Eisenhower was president, and he would be followed by John F. Kennedy, who would be assassinated, and then by Lyndon B. Johnson.

My birth was just about three years after the US Supreme Court handed down its landmark unanimous decision on Brown vs. Board of Education on May 17, 1954, declaring state laws that established separate public schools for whites and blacks unconstitutional.

"Separate educational facilities are inherently unequal," the Court declared.

Still, while the ruling technically outlawed segregation, enforcing it was a different matter.

In the year I was born, Governor Orval Faubus of Arkansas attempted to block black students from entering Little Rock Central High School, and in 1963, when I was 6, Governor George Wallace of Alabama stood in the doorway at the University of Alabama's Foster Auditorium to prevent two black students from enrolling.

"Segregation now. Segregation tomorrow. Segregation forever," he defiantly declared.

The governor would not step aside until forced to do so by the Alabama National Guard under orders from President Kennedy.

In the struggle to truly end segregation and gain equal rights for blacks, there were sit-ins by blacks and their allies at whites-only lunch counters, freedom rides and marches, riots, en-masse jailing of civil rights proponents, and even lynchings of blacks. In 1955, 14-year-old Emmett Till was brutally murdered in Mississippi for speaking to a white woman in a store. On September 15, 1963, Ku Klux Klan members blew up a church in Birmingham, Alabama, killing four young black girls and injuring twenty-two other people. Several black civil rights leaders were assassinated: Medgar Evers in 1963, Malcolm X in 1965, and Martin Luther King Jr. in 1968—all shot down in the prime of their lives.

Many people in this nation wanted to keep blacks "in their place," by any means necessary. They did not want us to rise.

The nation was also a battleground for women's rights in the 1960s and '70s. Women were still second-class citizens in many ways, and many people wanted to keep us "in our place." That sometimes meant "barefoot and pregnant." It sometimes meant "paid less for the same work." And it sometimes meant that they did not want women to rise above a certain level in the workplace.

As a young black woman growing up in the United States in the 1960s and '70s, I therefore knew that I had two strikes against me when it came to pursuing an education, a career, and any dreams I had.

In *African American Women with Disabilities: An Overview* (1992), Eddie Glenn calls attention to the disparate treatment of black women with disabilities, suggesting that a triple jeopardy syndrome puts us at a disadvantage because we are victims of race, gender, and disability bias in our society. In her research on the subject, she found that African American women with disabilities contributed disproportionately to the population of undereducated American women, were least likely to have high-school diplomas, did not vigorously participate in the labor force because of the severity of their disabilities, and were least likely to be married or living in family arrangements. In other words, the deck was stacked against us.

I was already generally aware of all of this. Therefore, over the years, if I didn't get a job I was qualified for, I had to wonder if it was because I am black, a woman, or have a disability. Or was there simply a better candidate? The truth is that I couldn't always know, and even if I did know, what could I really do about it?

For one thing, my conversations with the department head at Syracuse and the man who interviewed me for the broadcasting internship I didn't get taught me that I needed to develop my strengths further and make myself more competitive for getting what I wanted out of life. I realized that I would need to become so qualified that no one could turn me down in the future. I would have to somehow make myself that valuable.

19

Just One Look

Economic disadvantages were just a part of the problem. Being black and/or disabled was also a "problem" in other areas.

Looks seem to have always been important to people, and the "ideal look" especially in those days, was the look of a white woman, not a black woman. The white woman's skin color, hair, and facial and body type were considered more attractive, and some black women, although few would admit it today, tried to find a way to get closer to these "ideals." Popular—and mostly artificial—ways of doing this were altering their hair by straightening it and/or adding weaves or extensions; having plastic surgery; bleaching their skin; and losing weight. Unfortunately, this false standard of beauty also negatively impacted the psyche of many black women and made them feel that their self-worth was dependent on their physical appearance and a type of look that they usually could not attain.

Fortunately, many other black women did not feel the need to look like white women and were satisfied with the way they looked.

Regardless of how black women responded to this societal ideal, however, it still had the potential to affect us. For example, when a company wanted a model or actress, would it be more likely to choose a white model or actress who fit the "ideal" or a black model or actress who did not, except for limited types of projects? Even if hiring for a front-office receptionist job, would a company be more likely to choose the white "ideal" or the black woman, especially several decades ago?

Other people's perceptions of my attractiveness and femininity in relation to my missing leg and my limp also had an impact on me and often made me feel marginalized.

Of all the issues confronting women with disabilities, sexuality is perhaps the most charged. It is rather comical and equally disturbing how folks—both men and women—view me as a woman with a disability when it comes to sexuality. Women, for example, want to know how I can attract a man, while men are entertained by the idea that because I have one leg, sex with me must be a blast.

Several years after my amputation, when I was about 22, I found myself in a heated conversation with a female rival for a man's attention. In anger, she told me that I was less than a woman because I had only one leg.

"Why would he want you?" she told me. "You are not even a full woman."

During our argument, her taunt had hurt. Even though I wanted to deny it, the reality was that I had sometimes felt that way myself. Yet hearing it come from someone else's mouth was unexpected, shocking.

Finally, I pulled myself together and answered "Miss Thing."

At this point, our argument had become more than a rivalry over a man's love. For me, it had become a battle for my self-esteem.

I finally rallied and said, "How can you say that? Have you lived in my shoes, experienced what I've experienced? Are you some kind of expert on disabilities? And what's a leg got to do with it anyway? Even with just one leg, I'm more woman than you'll ever be!"

Finally, she shut up, and the argument ended. A little while later, she left the party with the man we'd been fighting over. As she walked out the door with him, she looked over her shoulder at me and flaunted her victory.

Afterward, of course, I went home and played the argument over in my head many times, thinking about what she had said and wondering if it might be true. Was I indeed less than a full woman? I mean, I had lost our competition for the man, after all. Didn't that prove her point?

Comments like the one from this rival prove the influence of negative stereotypes that suggest that women are the sum of their body parts.

Other misconceptions about women with disabilities include the following: that they are asexual or celibate, that they cannot handle sexual relationships, that they cannot be mothers, that they are all heterosexual, that they should be grateful for sexual relationships, that they are different, and that youth and beauty are essential to sexuality.

My personal experience and knowledge of these stereotypes and misconceptions are deeply rooted in my psyche, reminding me of the powerful impact of our socialization and indoctrination to look "normal." Reluctantly, I accept that there are men and women who have a "virus" that I have named the negative socialization virus (NSV), which socializes them to adopt negative beliefs and stereotypes about women who are physically different.

Unfortunately, when women are barraged with negative messages about our imperfect bodies—and our culture tells us that no matter how lovely we are, there is always something to improve—there is a strong likelihood that we will accept and internalize these unrealistic standards.

20

Open Wounds

"A broken bone can heal, but the wound a word opens can fester forever."

—Jessamyn West

Even several years after my amputation, my self-esteem and body image were still getting hit from every direction—from the general public, from men, from women, and from potential employers.

Remember the old saying "Sticks and stones may break my bones, but words will never hurt me"? Our parents often tell us this when others say something bad to us. It is an attempt to convince us that we aren't hurt by what others say like we would be if they actually hit us. Unfortunately, this saying is one of the biggest falsehoods that our parents tell us.

The truth is that, in most cases, being beaten physically only affects us for a short time until the physical wounds heal. On the other hand, when we are beaten emotionally with words from others, it sticks with us and affects us for a long time, perhaps even for life. When others tell us that we are ugly, stupid, worthless, or losers, or that we don't deserve success, we internalize those words and begin to believe them. These people's harsh words become, to some extent, our stories.

All of the negative words I heard plus my own internal feelings of loss, the shame I felt from other people's perceptions of me, the stigma attached to my disease and disability, and my fear of rejection kept bringing my focus back to my missing leg, my disability—*this one aspect* of who I was. As a result, I could only see what I had lost, not what I still had and all of my potential in other areas.

Unfortunately, in addition to the miserable internal feelings that people with a poor self-image, low self-esteem, and self-loathing have, there are also other negative results. If we perceive ourselves as valueless, unworthy, and/or failures, we might feel that there is no reason to try to rebuild our lives and might simply stop trying.

We may also acquire overeating/undereating disorders, become dependent on drugs or alcohol, become abusive or submissive to others in unhealthy relationships, suffer loneliness, be unable to form or maintain positive relationships, and/or develop personality disorders. Ultimately, our misery might lead us to depression and thoughts of suicide. Although we might try to overcome our problems through drug or alcohol abuse, promiscuity, perfectionism, or "fixing" our outer selves with fancy clothes or nice cars or houses, unless we fix the underlying self-image and self-esteem problems, we are still likely to be unsatisfied and unhappy with our lives.

■ ■ ■

When I met Richard and Noah during my time in Houston and they were attracted to me even though I was an amputee, I was encouraged that men I didn't know or have previous relationships with were showing interest in me.

I thought, Wow, I'm getting back to my stride! Men are attracted to me again. It was important at the time for helping rebuild my self-esteem.

When I was young—and to some extent even today—females were socialized to be pretty and dainty and to seek princes who would love us, marry us, and take care of us. So that idea was implanted in my brain.

In addition, I was always very much adored as a young girl. I was always considered pretty.

She's so pretty. She's so pretty. She's so pretty. That's all I heard.

My friends who knew me back then sometimes laugh and remind me of the type of little girl I was.

"My ribbons. My ribbons. Don't touch my ribbons. Look at me. Look at me," I would say.

As a result of the way others treated me and the excessive attention I received, I knew that I could have anybody I wanted, and anybody would want me. So when reality set in after I lost my leg, it was crushing. I had lost one of the main things I had going for me—my looks. I had been on a roll, and then the big crash came when I lost my leg and subsequently looked and walked different. I wasn't "the pretty girl" anymore.

The messages that I'd gotten from society very early were that if you look good, society treats you very well. And it's true. They do. Pretty people get things, and that's affirmed by the way many celebrities are treated. People who are considered unattractive in personality or looks generally don't get as much and aren't treated as well. They tend to not get as far; they're often ignored.

Since I grew up with those beliefs, and then people didn't want me anymore, I was like, "What do you mean you don't want me? I'll make you want me." So I used the most powerful weapon of all: sex. I thought if I gave men sex, they'd like me. Of course, I later realized that I had been a stupid girl. I understood later that they didn't like *me*. They liked *sex*. This is a valuable lesson, and girls need to understand it. If a man truly loves you, he will love the essence of you and not just be focused on sex. You shouldn't have to do that to be his focus. By understanding this reality, you can easily know who's really interested in you very quickly.

Unfortunately, I went through a period of promiscuous behavior before I realized this. Although I was sometimes reckless in college and experimented with smoking marijuana, I was never addicted and strung out. I was just experimenting and trying to find my way, but that type of self-destructiveness never really attracted me. Instead, I used sex because I felt inadequate. I didn't value myself and didn't make good decisions. I was determined to get validation from others. I was addicted to people telling me that I was pretty, that I was adored, and that they couldn't live without me. Although it was self-destructive, promiscuity was my way of trying to get those things back.

■　■　■

I realize now that sometimes it takes a crisis to humble people. Although this type of neediness—as exhibited through my promiscuous behavior—was humbling, I believe that the traumatic experience that led to it ultimately made me a better person. Of course, I wouldn't wish trauma on others, and I'm not saying a person has to lose a leg to be humbled, but if that's what has made me the person I am today, I'm happy that it happened because I think I'm a wonderful woman today with a wonderful soul and spirit. Before, I was very self-centered; I thought I was so special. I love myself now. Losing my leg has transformed my personality and my heart. It's much softer, kinder, more understanding, and more compassionate now. I think that's what we need more of today—more compassion for people.

This experience has also given me a passion to work with those less fortunate. I can definitely relate to them because I know what it feels like.

When I taught school, I worked with the overweight kids and the low-performing kids the most because I knew what life was going to be like for them. I saw it and experienced it. I can understand what bullying is like. I was bullied for being pretty when I was younger. I understand why others bullied me; when you're dogged all the time, you attack those who are getting the most attention.

When you look different, you're treated differently. And when you're a person with a disability, you really are treated differently, especially if you're a woman. It is blatant discrimination. Organizations and projects today that recognize and lift up women with disabilities are so significant because, for decades, women with disabilities were totally ignored. People didn't even think of us as being sexualized women. They would have never put the words "beautiful" and "disability" in the same sentence. No way. Fortunately, it's changing some now. The fashion industry is starting to embrace disability. Runways are starting to embrace it. We are showing up, and now disability is *en vogue*.

The legal protections regarding disability are also making some headway. The Americans with Disabilities Act (ADA) still has some room for improvement, but the treatment of people with disabilities in the past was horrible. People with developmental disabilities used to be institutionalized and locked away in "idiot cages," and people with physical disabilities didn't fare much better. Social rejection was an everyday occurrence. Although we still need to make significant improvements, we've definitely come a long way since those days.

21

A New Start

During my time in Syracuse, my relationship with Noah ended terribly. Long story.

Now that I was back in DC, I was ready to try to break into the communications industry again.

Since I could no longer afford to work without a paycheck, I took a job as a receptionist at USA Today in 1984. I had decided to gamble and take a low-level job with the company just to get my foot in the door since I hadn't completed enough coursework in journalism to be hired in the newsroom. I hoped that once I got inside the company, I could move up.

As planned, I quickly distinguished myself and was given various editorial assignments. Then USA Today's parent company, Gannett, started a division called Videotext, which predated the Internet. I was hired as a news assistant, and one of my duties was to organize and classify the newsroom resource library for electronic newsroom users. My strategy seemed to be working.

While I was thrilled to have this opportunity despite having to begin my day at 4:30 a.m., I quickly grew tired of the grueling hours. I began to hate the job and asked the company if there was something else I could do.

"Yes," I was told, "but you have to go to New York City for training."

New York! All right! Moving to The Big Apple sounded exciting to me.

My new job was in the circulation division, and I thought that I was so lucky to get it.

Unfortunately, this job did not appeal to me either. It was considered a major job, but it was just not me. I had to count the number of trucks and how many newspapers they had on them, and I hated it. I had a bachelor's degree in education and was close to completing my master's degree, but now I was working at a national media company without a journalism degree. In this job, my education meant nothing. I felt that my education was being wasted.

As a result, I decided to try to change jobs again.

"OK," the manager agreed, "we'll move you. You'll go back to DC and work in production."

Wow, I thought. This is great. Unfortunately, I did not research the finer details of the job. Little did

I know that production meant working in the pre-press phase, where the pages of the newspapers are laid out and designed in a composing area. It was manual labor! I had to stand on a rubber mat for long hours and use an X-Acto knife to cut out the print of the newspaper. I had totally misunderstood. I thought "production" was going to be a job on the newspaper similar to the job of a "producer" for TV news. I thought it was a professional job, but it was manual labor again, and I couldn't handle so many hours standing on my leg.

I thought I was so grand with my higher education, and I never thought it would turn out to be that kind of job. I actually showed up for the first day of work dressed to the nines, ready to produce some news, and found everyone else wearing jeans and sneakers. It was so embarrassing; I looked so out of place. I thought I had been promoted to the newsroom, and here I was in the composing room. It was a total disappointment—another job that I couldn't handle.

Ultimately, the management got tired of my complaining and said that I wasn't doing my job correctly. And I probably wasn't because I couldn't stand that long, and I couldn't sit.

I had been so excited to get the job and return to DC. The circulation job was more prestigious, and my friends had said, "How can you give this up to go to production?" But I thought I was going to be a producer, and it was all about the title for me. I was always mesmerized by the idea that I would be famous, and that's what production sounded like to me.

Anyway, the company was unwilling to accommodate me, and at that time, "reasonable accommodation" for people with disabilities wasn't required. Back then, a company could just get rid of somebody, and I was fired.

I filed a discrimination lawsuit with the Equal Employment Opportunity Commission (EEOC), but unfortunately, I was not successful at proving that I was discriminated against because of my race. Since it was before The Americans with Disabilities Act (ADA), my disability could not be raised as the cause of my being fired.

This experience was heartbreaking, and I thought it was the end for me.

These disappointments were starting to wear on my psyche, and I was beginning to wonder if maybe I was not good enough—that I was a fraud. Was I suffering from imposter syndrome, a term coined in the 1970s by psychologists and researchers to informally describe people who are unable to internalize their accomplishment, despite external evidence of their competence? African American women with disabilities are at particular risk for developing imposter syndrome given the mounting denials and rejections imposed on them in academia and the workforce. And it certainly didn't help when Supreme Court justice Antonin Scalia seemed to suggest in 2015 that many blacks belong at "slower" colleges.

Fortunately, I was able to move forward despite my self-doubt and the doubts of others. I still cared about my voice and continued to work on it. I went to voice classes and was encouraged when I would speak. I then decided that I would take this ability that I had that no one else seemed to recognize and extrapolate from it. That's when I transferred my dream of communications and performing to my teaching career again.

Above:
George Wallace, my junior high school prom date (circa 1972).

Top to bottom:
My high school sweetheart and prom date, Louis Graves.
Graduation day from Howard D. Woodson Senior High
School (1974). I'm standing on the terrace of the John F.
Kennedy Center for the Performing Arts, Washington, DC.

Top to bottom:
Standing outside Letts Hall at American University (AU) in
Washington, DC, feeling insecure because it was my first week
returning to campus after recovering from my surgery and I
was wearing a temporary prosthesis (circa 1977).
At an AU class picnic after a chemotherapy treatment.

Above: On a class field trip to the zoo during
my first year teaching (1979).

Part II

Sorting the Broken Pieces

22

Whatever It Takes

When I was younger, probably from the time I was 7 until I was 10, I remember many nights hearing my mother and father arguing loudly, mostly on the weekends when my father probably had one too many beers after working the midnight shift on his part-time job. These arguments could last for hours and were harsher in tone than the ones my youngest sister and I would have over clothes, socks, ribbons, toys, and lunch bags.

I never thought of my parents as alcoholics, however, because they only drank and became out of control on the weekends. They were like many people who might not meet the accepted criteria for being diagnosed as alcoholics but fall into the gray area of "problem drinkers."

Still, I survived the noisy nights and fiery arguments of that period of my life largely though my farfetched imagination. I remember reading fairytales as a way to escape, and I guess they contributed to my dreams of the future—of my wanting to be a princess, then a star, and then wanting to get my doctorate.

■ ■ ■

My parents divorced when I was in the seventh grade, and my mother, my youngest sister, and I eventually moved to a moderate-size, two-bedroom apartment on the third floor of an older three-story building in what would be considered an upper-lower-class section of Southeast Washington, DC, even despite my father's financial contributions to our household. Even though there was only a few-thousand-dollars difference between family income where I grew up and the area we moved to, the difference was obvious to me and seemingly to those who lived in other sections of the District of Columbia. When I would share with some families who lived in certain parts of Northwest DC that I lived in Southeast, there seemed to be an attitudinal shift. Some people who lived in Northwest looked down on people who lived in Southeast. I seemed to have internalized the class and income bias as well, and when I moved there from a better neighborhood, it was a letdown for me.

My friend John Bing, who lived across the street from me, now recalls me as a very outgoing, personable, and charismatic girl, who always knew what I wanted and was very self-assured.

"Very rarely do you find that," John says, "and in Southeast DC, expectations weren't very high. None of our parents had actually gone to college, and it was not really expected [that we would]."

He recalls, however, that I was very focused on getting out of the neighborhood and venturing off to college.

"When we were growing up," John recalls, "we had an integrated neighborhood, but later there was a lot of 'white flight.' John Kennedy, Martin [Luther King], and Robert Kennedy got killed, and we weren't sure who we were at that time, but Donna Walton knew. She just had that self-assurance."

■ ■ ■

I attended Carter G. Woodson Junior High School in the early 1970s, and our teachers there reflected the talent and learnedness of the man the school was named to honor. Carter Godwin Woodson was one of the first scholars to study African American history, and in 1926, he announced the celebration of Negro History Week, which is considered the predecessor of Black History Month. He is considered by some to be the father of black history.

One of my favorite teachers there was my seventh-period English teacher, Mrs. Geraldine Harper, who, along with my mother, was instrumental in fostering my educational aspirations.

During this stage, I identified many of my likes and dislikes. Although I enjoyed art class, I was *very* passionate about music class. Mrs. Harper also helped me hone my writing and speaking talents. I wrote short stories, poems, and plays, and my public speaking ability was discovered when I delivered my first speech for my campaign for class vice president and was later asked to represent the school at an official meeting organized by the Future Business Leaders of America. It was a big deal, and I thought I was too.

Later, at Howard D. Woodson Senior High, I was always in the process of trying to perfect myself. Though many of my insecurities were under control and I considered myself attractive to boys, I agonized over my appearance. As a result, I was constantly in conflict with jealous girls who seemed to despise me for both my looks and my confidence. Luckily, in senior high, I did not encounter girls like Barbara, the girl who literally came to my house to beat me up during the summer before I entered seventh grade.

"You brag too much," she said.

She then threw a punch, and, unlike most fighters, I began talking my way out of the next blow. I could not bear the thought of a marked-up face from her fingernails, so I bargained with her and told her that I would let her tell the boys in our class that she beat me up.

I always knew that I wanted to be great and famous, although at first I didn't have a clue how—whether I'd be a singer, a dancer, or an actor. No one really cultivated these dreams or any talents that I had. I just went forth on my own.

After my amputation, when I started reinventing my life, I knew for sure that I didn't want to be an alcoholic or a drug user and that I didn't want a life filled with physical, emotional, or any other kind of abuse.

I think that perhaps part of my later decision to pursue the highest level of education was to ensure that I could avoid the type of lives I'd seen others in my neighborhood and family fall into—lives that included alcoholism, substance abuse, domestic abuse, and poverty.

I had wanted more for my life before I had the amputation, and I was not going to settle for less afterward. I knew what a determined person I was, and I was willing to do whatever it took once I knew what I wanted. Though I didn't have a clear vision, I knew that I wanted my life to be positive, to be motivational to others, and to make a difference.

23

Ball of Confusion

"Growth is painful. Change is painful. But nothing is as painful as staying stuck somewhere you don't belong."

—Mandy Hale

"Obstacles are those frightful things you see when you take your eyes off the goal."

—Henry Ford

Unfortunately, the '80s was a difficult decade for me as I continued to try to find my way in the world. I was still evolving and adjusting to life as an amputee and living in fear that the cancer might return.

It was also depressing when I had to start over after several failed relationships. This would mean having to go through the motions of sharing who I was—an amputee—with someone new and having to experience rejection if he was not prepared to date a girl who limped and wore an artificial leg.

My life was full of confusion, and unfortunately, during this period, I didn't always make great decisions. I flipped and flopped between relationships, was in a constant search for the perfect job, and vacillated between wanting to pursue teaching and abandoning my dream. I was not quite sure what I was looking for.

During this period, I began to flirt with same-sex relationships. In fact, I found such comfort and refuge with women that I did not date any men for an extended period of time. With women, there was less judgment, and I felt much more liberated. Still, although I began to thrive in some areas of my life from time to time, I experienced many emotional ups and downs and was by no means truly happy.

At times, I would feel positive and begin to get my life back to where I wanted it, and at other times, I would fall or get knocked down by my own insecurities, others' negative attitudes, or failed relationships. Although I caused a lot of my own problems, a lot of them were also caused by others as, from time to time, I encountered a variety of toxic people. These included "dreambusters," "naysayers," "energy vampires," "procrastinators," and "people infected with NSV."

At times, these people threatened to destroy both my confidence and my soul.

The dreambusters are those who to tell us that our dreams are impossible, that we're not able to accomplish them. These people don't believe in dreams and have no faith or hope. As a result, they try to also take away our faith and hope.

The naysayers are those who are always giving advice, and it is always negative advice. They expect us to fail and tell us so.

The critics are those who always seem to find problems with what we do. Whatever we do, it's not quite good enough in their eyes.

The energy vampires suck our energy away with their negativity and leave us drained and unmotivated.

The procrastinators sometimes come in the guise of friends telling us that we can put things off until another time.

The people with NSV are those who still refer to people with developmental disabilities as "retarded" or who mock people who are deaf and mute by referring to them as "deaf and dumb." These people have not learned to embrace difference rather than fear it.

Unfortunately, even today, it seems that not a week goes by without my being confronted by folks who are infected with NSV. I run into them in the subway, at the grocery store, in the elevator, at concerts, and in schools and religious institutions.

These destructive people are everywhere, and the more we allow them to invade our lives, the more they can infect us with their poison and rob us of our possibilities. It may take years or even decades to recover from their harm. In my opinion, these people and their impact can be far worse than cancer. I beat cancer, but I am still battling the residual effects of such toxic people today.

That others are going to judge us and find fault with us is pretty much a given. Sad, but true. And it's also pretty much a given that we have no control over anyone else's thoughts about us.

So what can we do to protect ourselves?

We can avoid these people as much as possible, and if we must hear their words, we can ignore them and move on, refusing to let them affect us. It is not easy, I know, but we must keep in mind how destructive such words are—and that they are often nothing more than opinions anyway. Unfortunately, sometimes these toxic people are among our closest friends and relatives, which makes it more difficult to avoid or ignore them. But we must if we are to save ourselves.

It is also important to recognize that we can be our own dreambuster, naysayer, energy vampire, procrastinator, or person infected with NSV. While we might be blaming others and our life situation for the obstacles in our lives that are stopping us from fulfilling our dreams, a closer analysis might reveal that they are actually a result of our own negative attitudes, beliefs, or actions.

■   ■   ■

After my years at USA Today and Gannett, I became an adjunct faculty member at Trinity College in Washington, DC, where I taught graduate-level courses in special education for about a year. In addition, for most of that time, I was also an education coordinator/manager at Wave, Inc. At Wave, I implemented and supervised a computerized vocational curriculum for disadvantaged youths and adults. My efforts resulted in my promotion to program manager, supervising job counselors in their efforts to obtain jobs for out-of-school youths.

After that, I was project director for the National Association of Partners in Education in nearby Alexandria, Virginia. There, I directed, managed, and marketed a federal drug-abuse-prevention program. My role included the coordination of a national conference and twenty-six nationally mobilized community coalitions.

Looking for an opportunity to relocate, I was hired as a program development specialist for the

East Coast Migrant Head Start Project (ECMHSP), which was headquartered in Arlington, Virginia. The ECMHSP provided services to migrant farmworkers and their children in twenty-six Head Start centers in Alabama, Florida, North Carolina, South Carolina, and Virginia. Guess where I relocated? I had a beautiful setup in Boca Raton, Florida, with e-mail and a home copier before these things became common. This position offered me a great opportunity to work largely from home in the early Internet days

My main role was developing adult education training for teachers, staff, and managers on appropriate early childhood education practices for migrant farmworkers' children.

Unfortunately, I also had to travel throughout Florida to train the staff and directors of these Head Start centers, which were located near rural migrant labor camps. The problem was that I had to drive long distances to these centers and would have to stay overnight in hotels that were located in remote areas of town. It was scary and dangerous to be out on those roads alone without a phone. This was in the pre-cell-phone days, and although there were car phones, they were extremely expensive

"I really need a car phone for this job for my safety," I told my boss one day. "Driving in rural areas and on back roads alone is so potentially dangerous if my car breaks down, especially at night."

My supervisor apologized but said that giving me a phone would be impossible because if they gave me one, every employee would expect one, and they couldn't afford that.

This was before the ADA passed and gave people with disabilities some protections. Pre-ADA, no one was thinking about accommodating people with disabilities. If you got the job, you were expected to work the job just like everybody else.

So, here I was, a black woman with a disability driving long distances on isolated back roads in the rural South at night. So I got angry. I didn't care if no one else got a phone. I needed one for my safety.

That phone became an issue, and I realized that this job was not going to work out for me and began to cast my net for something new. This would turn out to be one of the "losses" that would ultimately move me forward toward higher education.

Since I loved Florida and didn't want to leave the state, I applied for a position at Boca Elementary School and got the job. This enabled me to remain in Florida and decide what my next move would be.

Throughout this period, I was ready to constantly move and take risks with my career, and that helped me continue striving to reinvent myself, although I didn't think of it like that at the time.

24

What You Know and Who You Know

Although my love life was going through ups and downs—mostly downs—I did get some great news for my career. After teaching at Boca Elementary School for about a year, I landed a position as a faculty member at Miami Dade Community College, now named Miami Dade College, on the medical center's campus. I taught basic composition courses for the Developmental Studies Department and served as resource to the Disabled Student Support Services Department.

■　■　■

On more than one occasion, I learned that both *what* you know and *who* you know are important. Valerie Boyd, who I met on my first pilgrimage to Eatonville, Florida, to attend a Zora Neale Hurston Festival, shared my name with Dr. Beverly Guy-Sheftall, head of the Women's Research and Resource Center at Spelman College, which happened to have funding from the Ford Foundation to train faculty on disability awareness and sensitivity toward students with disabilities. Thanks to *what* I knew and *who* I knew, I was paid for my second consulting job. (My first payment for consulting was years earlier during my first year of teaching at the Houston Independent School District when I was hired to create an educational curriculum for students who were transitioning from the court system to the school system.)

Years earlier, in 1986, I had used home video equipment to produce a film documenting myths and misconceptions about people with disabilities. I had hoped to use it to educate teachers, principals, rehabilitation professionals, and parents of children with disabilities on the impact of disabilities in people's lives. Unfortunately, disability was not a central topic at the time, so obtaining funding to produce the video was extremely difficult.

In 1995, almost ten years later and still undeterred from my goal of educating others about disabilities, I successfully struggled to convince colleges and universities in Florida and Georgia that they should have a "Disability Awareness Day." As a result, I was finally able to write, narrate, direct, and produce a video for the Disabled Student Support Services Department at Miami Dade. With this, as well as another educational video I created for female amputees, I was able to impact the lives and perspectives of many people. Additionally, I presented workshops to faculty and administrators on disability-sensitivity and -awareness practices. These activities led to my promotion to writing coordinator for the Developmental Studies Department.

While I was teaching at Miami Dade, I also inspired one of my students, Heriberto Gonzales, to write an article about my influence on his thinking about people with disabilities. In summer 1993, his article, "They Seek Not Your Pity," was published in *THE ANTIDOTE* (Volume 16, Number 6). At the beginning of his article, Heriberto says that when I first told him about my amputation, he felt sorry for me. At the end of his article, however, he wrote these words: "Before feeling sympathy for people with disabilities, you should remember: they seek not your pity, but your understanding and respect."

This article helped me realize that my story could influence others and made me begin to think more about my future role in helping people overcome many of the difficulties in their lives.

This idea grew even stronger in 1994 when my first article "What's a Leg Got to Do With It?" was published by *HealthQuest*, the first nationally distributed magazine focusing on the health of African Americans. Valerie Boyd, one of the magazine's co-founders, who also functioned as its editor in chief, had been an inspiration to me and had encouraged me to write the article for the magazine. An author, journalist, cultural critic, and professor, Valerie is also the author of the critically acclaimed biography, *Wrapped in Rainbows: The Life of Zora Neale Hurston*.

25

Ain't No Mountain High Enough

"If what you want isn't behind Door Number 1, Door Number 2, or Door Number 3, don't settle for less. Knock a hole in the wall, and make a new door."

—DONNA R. WALTON

These words are a great summary of the concept of reinvention. For years, I had been going from job to job, entering door after door. Unfortunately, as I entered those doors, sometimes merely because they were easy to enter, I often found out that I didn't really want to be there. I was settling. In the '90s, however, that really started to change.

■ ■ ■

"Should I go for a doctoral degree or not?" I asked myself over and over in 1995. I loved my position at Miami Dade Community College, but I began to realize that if I wanted to grow academically and professionally, I needed to go for higher learning. I also loved South Florida and realized that if I wanted to own something there on the beach, I would need more money than my current salary.

I knew that I wasn't getting any younger, but at my age (then 38), it was not a decision to be made lightly. I had a cushy job, and things were going fairly well in my life. Why give up security and relative peace and exchange it for the life of a student and financial struggle?

In the end, I made the decision to pursue my doctorate. My mother had always encouraged me and my sister to get as much education as we could, and by now I was coming to grips with the reality that I would not be living out my dreams in Hollywood.

People were also beginning to ask me to share my experiences with others, and I did not want to do so based on my life experiences alone. I wanted to provide greater value to those I spoke to, and I thought that my talks and presentations would have more credibility if I had higher academic credentials.

When I finally made up mind to pursue my doctoral degree, the lyrics to the megasong "Ain't No Mountain High Enough," written by Nickolas Ashford and Valerie Simpson, were my mantra. And I could hear its melody reverberate in my brain like an irate Ping-Pong ball as I sat at a wide conference table with the chair of the counseling program during my preadmission interview.

"You know it's going to take you many years to complete this degree," he explained. "You must consider the number of prerequisite courses you would have to take since your master's is not in counseling."

His counsel was familiar to my ears, so I was prepared with my rebuttal and was determined to make my dreams come true and his words become moot.

Time will pass no matter how long it takes to finish and whatever age I am so I might as well do something, I recall thinking as I listened to him continue to caution me about the rigors of starting such a program at my late age.

"Regardless of how long it takes and no matter what age I will be," I told him, "I will earn my degree, and I will be Dr. Walton for the rest of my life."

■　■　■

So in summer 1995, I ended my full-time faculty position at Miami Dade Community College, moved to a less-expensive apartment in DC, entered The George Washington University (GW) doctoral program in counseling, and dove into the books with other students who were mostly about ten years younger than me.

Before beginning my doctoral classes in the fall, however, I also took a position in the Writing Laboratory at Bowie State University in Bowie, Maryland. My role was mainly to assist students with their composition assignments using computer-assisted instruction (CAI).

My advisor at GW, Jorge Garcia, was very encouraging and helped me decide that I wanted to specialize in rehabilitation counseling. In my second year, I told him that I wanted to do research in the area of counseling female amputees across their lifespans and that I wanted to subspecialize in career counseling. Because of my continuing interest in the situation of African American female amputees, earlier in my doctoral studies, I submitted a research proposal to the National Institutes of Health (NIH) to seek funding. The proposal, titled "A Black Female Amputee Rehabilitation Education Model," aimed to develop and test an intervention designed specifically to help a segment of this population develop coping styles that would lead to better psychosocial adjustment to their disabilities. I was really gaining a profound interest in working with women with disabilities at this time, and there was clearly a void in the research.

Although I was not awarded the funding for the proposed project, it was an excellent learning opportunity and motivator. My efforts proved that I was smart and that my disability had nothing to do with it.

■ ■ ■

Kamili Anderson, who worked at Howard University as an editor for *The Journal of Negro Education*, was a guiding light for me during this period. At the time, she always encouraged me to keep going and keep writing, and to reward me, she gave me an opportunity to write an article review.

I did it, and my article was published! My proverbial bonnet was starting to resemble a peacock's feathers.

I was really starting to get a clear understanding of where I wanted to be career-wise, although I wasn't quite able to get there yet.

■ ■ ■

I attended GW part time and full time, step by step, course by course, for the next ten years, while I also worked full time and gained experience. It was daunting. I sacrificed social outings, relationships, and almost all of my opportunities for leisure time. It would be faith, family, and friends that would light the path during this long and rigorous period.

The decision to go for my doctorate was another "game of life" decision, and I performed very well through all of the challenges it presented until I walked across the stage in May 2006, earning my EdD in rehabilitation counseling.

The feeling I had walking across the stage on graduation day was similar to the feeling I would have had if I were performing at Carnegie Hall. Once again, I realized that my preamputation dreams of singing, dancing, and performing had not been lost, only changed. *Final Act: "Earning My Doctoral Degree." Title:* Performing in the Wind. *The curtain closes. I turn the tassel, put down the microphone, turn left, and exit the stage.*

During this period, I was also an adjunct faculty member/teaching assistant in the Graduate School of Education and Human Development. I taught graduate-level courses, assisted in the implementation of a distance-learning course on disability case management, and provided technical assistance to special-education teachers and counselors on school-to-work transition activities. I was really honing my craft.

Although I had been concerned about returning to graduate school at such a late stage in my life, I now realize that my experiences as a woman with a disability were a valuable part of the educational experience for the other students. Many of them got a perspective on issues that they wouldn't have gotten if they hadn't had a person with my various characteristics and experiences in the class. I'm glad I was able to go back to school at my age, and I don't believe that anyone is too old to do so.

26

Reinventing Me

Since my amputation, I had been going through a major deconstruction of my old self, and a new me was being reconstructed. This process had been going on in bits and pieces for about twenty years, and even though I was getting closer to who and what I wanted to be—maybe even needed to be—the process was still not complete.

During this period, I had to think more deeply about who I was and who I was not. Then, I had to learn how to affirm myself—my new self.

As I mentioned earlier, one of the biggest problems with having our lives shattered is that it often destroys our self-image and self-esteem and, in some cases, even makes us hate ourselves. A major myth is that because of *this one problem*, we no longer have *any* value—that we are worthless, that we are losers. We tend to become so laser-focused on *the one thing* we feel we've lost or have "failed" at that we forget all of the things we still have and all of our positive qualities.

My laser focus on my lost leg made me miserable. Before this loss, I had thought highly of myself. I had thought that because I was pretty, had a great shape, wore hip clothes, was liked by my peers, and had plenty of boyfriends and a main squeeze who wanted to marry me, I was something special. There was nothing in the world that I believed I could not do. I had all a teenage girl wanted or needed to love herself and her life.

Until the day I lost my leg.

This loss, in my perception, changed *everything*.

It seemed that this loss had stripped away *everything* of value in my life, and I felt like just giving up at times.

A lot of my reinvention was not an intentional process. In hindsight, I can describe my journey with the appropriate psychological terms and analyses, but at the time, I just did it. Somewhere, from deep down in that part of me that only God knows, lurked the inclination to move toward wholeness and tap into the personal power that was already there waiting for the moment when I needed it most. Our *selves* often work this way. Some parts of us seem to be designed to activate when others no longer serve us properly.

Although this was purely a self-directed psychological process, it was very powerful. Despite all of the negativity that invaded my environment, my thinking, and, at times, my very being, I somehow "knew" that everything was going to be OK—more than OK—at some point and that I could trust my intuition. Fortunately, that intuition told me to flood my mind with nothing but more aspirations, dreams, and goals and to be positive. In fact, I became obsessed (possessed if you will) with positivity. This, I somehow knew, was the key to overriding the nightmare.

I realized that I had a choice. I could allow the accidental authors of negativity to write the story of who I was—a crippled girl, Poor Donna—or I could claim the right to write my own story and establish my own image. I, of course, chose the latter. I could not accept that I had lost the power to claim who I was in the world—that such a power had been somehow assigned to other people. Who knew better who I was and what I had the potential to be than me?

Also, once I finally began to realize that negativity and self-hatred were not going to get me the "happy" that I wanted in my life, I began to ask myself an important question—a question that would truly change my life: What's a leg got to do with it?

In reality, it was as much a statement as a question.

Ultimately, I realized that my life was not defined by whether I had that leg or not.

This simultaneous question and affirmation became one of my strongest mottos, and it still is today. "What's a leg got to do with it?" My answer then and now: "Absolutely nothing!"

I finally realized that I had intrinsic value whether I had two legs or not. I knew that I was more than the sum of my body parts. More than a single aspect. I was much more than a leg. I was a full person.

Just as novelist Terry McMillan's character Stella in *How Stella Got Her Groove Back* lost her groove and got it back when she fell in love with a fine, young Jamaican man, I lost my leg and got my groove back when I fell in love with myself.

Only when I learned to love myself could I really begin developing the new me that I really wanted to be.

Along with all of this, I came to realize another truth: I wasn't physically challenged as much as I was challenged by *other people's perceptions*. In fact, the physical loss of my leg was nothing compared to dealing with the negative ways that people perceived me.

Nothing had changed externally. People still stared, and a stigma against people with disabilities still existed. People still rejected me. The change was internal. My perception of myself had changed, and that made all the difference. Once I got my focus off that leg, it was as if I had once been blind and then gained 20/20 vision. I could now see my many other positive qualities, skills, and talents.

Building—or rebuilding—a positive self-image and high self-esteem is an individual project that we must ultimately accomplish within *ourselves*. While it is nice to have, validation from *others* cannot heal our souls once they become sick and malnourished. The inner spirit is the proper nourishment for our self-image and self-esteem, just like food and water are proper nourishment for the body. When we try to nourish our self-image and self-esteem with the wrong things, it will not work and might even poison us.

Take, for example, a woman who seems to have it going on. She has the perfect body, a great income, a fashionable wardrobe, and excellent health, yet this woman does not think well of herself. So what does she do? She seeks outside approval and temporary, superficial feel-goods. Determined to feel better about herself, she tries to feed her soul with casual sex, expensive shopping sprees, too much food and alcohol, substance abuse, and so on. Unfortunately, these things will never enhance her self-image and self-esteem for the long term and might simply produce a higher tolerance for superficial things. She might buy something because she believes that it will make her feel good. She might then buy something else that she thinks will make her feel better. And when she still needs more, she might buy something else. And yet none of it will satisfy her for long; it will ultimately only make her feel worse about herself.

I repeat: A thirsty, dying soul cannot feed on the *outside*; it must be fed from the *inside* with positive affirmations against fear, doubt, stress, and unworthiness.

As I asserted my need to set standards of womanhood and beauty for myself and to develop my new soul, I began laying the foundation of two of the principles that I continue to draw on today: Live authentically, and live by your own values.

As several people have been reported to have said, "If you don't know where you're going, you will probably end up somewhere else."

My life had been like this. Although I had goals and aspirations after my amputation, I didn't have the goals and aspirations that were 100 percent *true to myself*—my *authentic* self. Therefore, I was continually ending up not quite where I wanted to be—or should be.

"Authenticity" and "living an authentic life" have been defined in different ways by different philosophers, but I define them for myself as "being true to my own core principles and values rather than just following societal norms and letting others pressure me into things that don't fit my core principles, desires, and goals." In other words, as Shakespeare wrote, "To thine own self be true."

Many people who have achieved some unique success in life are familiar with this principle. Oprah, the late Steve Jobs, and others like them wouldn't have gotten as far as they did without drawing on something deep down that helped them decide that they could make their way in the world as themselves and not as somebody else's idea of who they should be. Like them, we have to be dedicated to painting our own picture and writing our own narrative about who—and what—we are. When we are trying to fulfill our mission, often without a clear road map to follow, old ways of thinking just won't do.

It took a lot of time and prayer to rewire my brain so that I could rewrite the story of my life, but I was now getting back on track.

With a renewed love for myself, I also finally got my mind right when it came to relationships. I now realized that to be a man or woman's "eye candy" was both flattering and fleeting and to be the "apple of someone's eye" was romantic, but to be wholesome in mind and spirit—to be genuine to my own authenticity—was real beauty.

I cannot say for certain what day it was that I actually stared at my full body in a mirror. For years,

I had relied on others to validate that my body was still beautiful—or at least acceptable. I do recall that it was just after I had taken a shower, and as I hopped on one leg across my bedroom, I stopped in front of a full-length mirror and stood balanced on my one leg. I was surprised by the beauty; my waist, my breasts, and my residual limb all seemed to come together for me, and I actually liked what I saw—the smooth skin of the residual limb, the perfect incision across its base.

I struck several poses and then made a few dance-like movements.

It was as if I had discovered a new me, a woman in my 30s who had not lost her balance, shake, or rhythm. When I began to see myself as beautiful again, I found myself dancing more in public, at parties, and at home. I was beginning to feel the freedom to really enjoy movement again.

My breakthrough from promiscuous behavior came from a combination of therapy, books, and God. I simply woke up one day and moved forward. I came to a point where, instead of vying for the acceptance of others, often through promiscuity, I started expecting *them* to convince *me* that they were worthy of me, and that is where I remain today. Once I regained my self-love, acquiring love from others was no longer that important.

I knew that finding my authentic self was not necessarily going to be easy, but I was even more willing now to work for it. And, fortunately, there are clues to whether or not we are living authentically. When we are not being authentic, we might feel out of character, out of flow, as if the things we are doing don't fit. On the other hand, when we are engaged in authentic living, things will likely feel more "right," more in flow, more true to character. For example, an authentic career path might be discovered by realizing the kinds of things we would do without being paid—just because we want to do them or feel that we *must* do them. And I began to see such things in my own life.

In order to know who we are and who and what we want to be—how we want to reinvent ourselves— we need to understand our core principles and desires. We can ask ourselves several questions that might help us:

- What do I love?
- What do I hate?
- What do I want to change about the world?
- What do I think about the most?
- What angers me the most?
- What makes me smile the most?

- What kinds of books, movies, and songs do I like?
- What would I do if I could do anything I want to?

If we love animals, for example, we might want to become a veterinarian. If we hate inequality, we might want to become a civil rights activist. If we think about cars all the time, we might want to be a mechanic or engineer. If we are angered by injustice in the world, we might want to become a politician. If children make us smile the most, we might want to become a children's book author, a teacher, a nanny, or a coach.

When our reinvented self is in line with our core principles and desires, we stand a greater chance of succeeding and of being happier with our life.

We might also want to ask others who know us well what they think would fit us. Then, once we've come up with an idea of who we are and who and what we want to be, we should look at that idea critically to determine if it is really right for us. To do so, we might ask ourselves the following questions:

- What will it take for me to reinvent myself like this?

- Am I willing to change in order to become this? How much am I willing to change or give up?
- Does the person I want to become align with my core principles and desires?
- Do I currently have what it takes to be this person, or will I have to learn new skills? Am I willing to put in the effort required to do so?
- Are there any conflicts between what I want to become and my current life? Can I somehow overcome these conflicts?
- Can I persevere until I reach success?
- Am I choosing this for the correct reason, or am I choosing it because someone else wants me to or because it offers a high salary?
- Is this what I really want for myself? If we can't answer yes to this question, we might need to take a little more time to make our decision.

Although we might want to listen to other people's opinions and consider them in our self-analysis, we should not let them or our situation define us. When we want to reinvent ourselves, we must do the defining. As Steve Jobs, co-founder of Apple, one of the most influential and well-known companies in history, said, "Your time is limited, so don't waste it living someone else's life."

Once these types of authentic things are discovered, we can start to build on them. However, to do so, we will need to make changes. As famed businessman and writer Max De Pree noted, "We cannot become what we need to be by remaining what we are" and "The greatest thing is, at any moment, to be willing to give up who we are in order to become all that we can be."

So unless we are already living an authentic life, we must leave some things behind in order to do so. The question for me was whether or not I was willing to give up where I was to get to where I wanted to be. My answer: Definitely!

Of course, I still had many ups and downs—but now it seemed the ups were far outnumbering the downs!

That's what loving oneself can do.

27

It All Comes Back to Teaching

On May 19, 1996, I wrote the following letter to myself:

> *Dear Donna.*
> *It is not necessary to worry about the things that you cannot change. Work on those things that you can.*

"Our nettlesome task," Dr. Martin Luther King Jr. said, "is to discover how to organize our strength into compelling power." While King's words were probably about organizing the strengths of many people in a movement to oppose grave racial injustice, the meaning is also powerful in respect to individuals and how we must each organize our personal strengths into compelling power. We all have strengths and weaknesses. By taking advantage of our strengths and combining them, we are more likely to find success.

I guess I knew either consciously or subconsciously that the person I would become would in some way or another still be a teacher. As a child, I was always curious, even nosy. I was a know-it-all and always believed that I had knowledge and that I should pass it on to others. In addition, most of my jobs and volunteer activities over the years were in teaching and/or working with people who were disenfranchised in some way, including truants, ex-offenders, and those with developmental disabilities.

For some reason, I seem to be predisposed to both teaching and working with those less fortunate than I am, and I really enjoy it. Perhaps it is because my race, gender, and disability often caused me to be disenfranchised in some way or another. No doubt, growing up during the battles for the rights of blacks, women, and those with disabilities influenced me as well.

Yes, I would be a teacher, but what form would that vocation take? The answer to that question was just around the bend.

Above: Photos of me wearing a dress for the first
time since my amputation surgery (circa 1980).

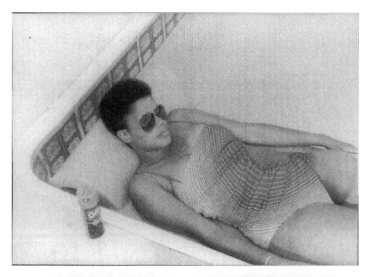

Clockwise from top: Wearing a bathing suit and in a swimming pool for the first time since my amputation surgery (circa 1985). Basking in the sun on a beach in Hollywood, Florida (1998). On the beach in Ocean City, Maryland (1990).

Part III

Making a Beautiful Mosaic

28

Reinventing You

The 2011 movie *The Adjustment Bureau* deals with various life themes, including "fate," who determines it, and whether or not it can be reset. Without getting into a heavy philosophical discussion of what fate is or a religious conversation about who determines it, I would like to share with you my belief about determining our own endgame—our own reinvention.

When I made the decision to come off chemotherapy—against the advice of my doctor, the love of family, and conventional wisdom—it represented a paradigm shift for me, a shift in thinking that gave me a say in my own endgame. I made that decision about forty years (or 350,400 hours) ago, yet I remember the very second I took control over my life.

I believe that you too can choose your endgame this very second—that there is a "yes" out there somewhere to whatever you want to do or become; all you have to do is make the adjustment. And what if you were meant to be doing exactly what you're doing, but it's not what you really want to do? Is our end-game totally subject to fate, or do we have a say in changing our present circumstances? In the movie, the two main characters are on separate tracks toward their predetermined success, and as long as they remain on track, things will end well; however, if they deviate from the course, they risk being reset by the Adjustment Bureau or losing out altogether. On the other hand, if they follow the preset course, they will also lose the chance to be together.

We hear all the time that life is short. Guess what—it gets shorter if you don't exercise the choices that are only yours to make. Many people are ready to write your story for you, but are you willing to let them? I wasn't.

29

Finding Our "Calling"

Teachers, philosophers, psychologists, and writers have used a variety of metaphors and similes to talk about the possibility of a new and better life that might await each of us. Some have talked about the caterpillar emerging from its cocoon as a butterfly. Others have spoken of the flower blooming from a bud. And yet others have envisioned a phoenix rising from the ashes of one that has died.

It's clear that thinkers have recognized that each of us has something inside us that wants to burst forth. In order to do so and emerge as something much more beautiful, however, it must first cast off the old shell that limits it. It may be a desire to be something or do something that we are not yet experiencing. You might already feel that something growing within you.

I especially like the metaphor of a clay pot being shattered and then the broken pieces being used to make a beautiful mosaic because it includes a strong element of *choice*. We can choose the picture we want for our life, and we can choose which pieces of the broken pot to include in making it. In this metaphor, each piece of the broken pot represents something negative or positive that we can throw out or keep to make our mosaic.

Historically, people have had a lot less choice about their lives and careers than we do today. They often had fewer choices about the person they could marry, and once they were married, they were often trapped. There was a greater stigma to divorce, and people were more likely to remain in "bad" marriages to avoid being stigmatized. It was especially difficult for women since their husbands were often the bread-winners and jobs for women were much more limited.

People also had fewer choices about employment. Men, and women if they worked outside the home, were often relegated to certain types of professions or jobs. If your father was a farmer, you would likely become a farmer. If your father was a blacksmith, you would likely become a blacksmith. Instead of going to college, you learned your father's profession. Some people might have had a little more choice by being an apprentice for someone in another profession, but still the choices were very limited.

Today, on the other hand—with thousands of colleges, universities, and training schools; with the availability of scholarships and financial aid; with the ability to work part-time and go to school; and with the ability to learn for ourselves with a library card or through a mentor—the possibilities are almost *un-limited*. It is also possible to change jobs and careers nowadays in ways that people couldn't easily do in the past. In fact, people today often change careers several times during their lifespan.

There is also less stigma attached to divorce. We women are in the workforce and can support ourselves and our children after divorce. If we don't make enough money, we might be able to get government assistance to help us survive during hard times. We are no longer trapped.

Although the situation is far from perfect, there clearly appears to be more opportunity to reinvent ourselves today than there was in the past. We have much more opportunity to leave behind the things that are no longer working for us.

Sometimes, if we look at our life and analyze it, we realize that we don't have a life that's simply *gone a little wrong*; instead, we have the *wrong life*. We don't have a *job with problems*; *our job is the problem*. We don't have a *relationship that has failed*; we have a *failure in the relationship we chose*.

Some people will analyze their lives and decide to give up everything and go for their dreams. Others might want to keep one foot in their current life and start testing the waters of their new one.

I want to make an important distinction here between *who we are* and *what we do*. When what we do defines who we are, we are often defining ourselves wrongly. For example, if I happen to get a job as a hair stylist, when people ask me about myself, I might say that I'm a hair stylist. However, that might merely be my job—something that I ended up doing with little planning or thought. It might have little to do with the core of my being.

However, when *who we are* defines *what we do*, our lives are generally where we want them to be. To make this happen, we must analyze ourselves and learn who we are, what we love and are passionate about, what concerns us, and what we want to accomplish. Once we know these things, we can choose our path based on them. If we love and are passionate about art, for example, we might become an artist, a graphic designer, an interior designer, a children's book illustrator, or something similar.

Another problem that can lead us down the wrong path is the mistaken belief that because we possess a certain skill, it should determine our life's work or purpose. For example, we might think that because we are good at writing, we should be a writer, editor, or publisher. Although being good at writing might help us in those jobs, it doesn't mean that they are the path we *should* pursue, because they might not be in line with our passions and what we love to do and want to accomplish. Instead, we might want to pursue a life in politics because we are passionate about helping others or we want to change the world. While writing skills will be helpful in this type of profession, they don't have to be central.

Finally, some of us choose to reinvent ourselves, and we come up with a vision of what we want, but we don't actually follow it. Perhaps we procrastinate, perhaps we are not committed enough, or perhaps we just don't know how to start.

One of the quotes that motivates me the most says, "If you want something in your life that you have never had, then you are going to have to do something that you have never done!" I don't know who first said this, and I don't know if it's an exact quote, but it's right on target. I also think that the word *do* should be emphasized. "You are going to have to *do* something that you have never done." Not *hope* something. Not *wish* something. Not *dream* something. Not *think* something. *Do* something.

Once we've decided we want to reinvent ourselves, we can begin the work of doing so. In fact, we *must* do the work. We can't reinvent ourselves just by *thinking* we are something else. We don't become a dancer, writer, expert mechanic, engineer, great salesperson, or artist by simply deciding to be that and thinking we are.

Some people say they want to be an artist or writer, but they hardly ever draw or paint or write. They go for months or years intermittently working on their projects. Are these people artists or writers? Probably not. The *idea* of being an artist or writer is what interests them. But the work? Not so much. However, the actual drawing, painting, or writing is what actually makes a person an artist or writer, not the dreaming about it. Real painters paint, and real writers write.

One artist I read about was very talented, but she had not been using her talent. Then, when she was 24, she committed to painting every day for one year. Today, Dana Tiger is a well-known artist whose amazing paintings of strong Native American women are displayed in universities, government buildings, and galleries. If she had not done the work, her talent might have been wasted. She might have been an artist in her soul, but no one would have known it, and the world would have missed the beautiful artwork she has produced over the years.

Another artist (or potential artist) I heard about was very talented, but he rarely drew or painted. He worked mostly odd jobs to support himself and often talked about establishing himself as an artist until he was in his mid-50s. During that time, he'd finish maybe one or two paintings a year. The ones he finished were well done, but it's difficult to establish a career with such little output. A few years later, this talented man died of cancer, and his unused talent tragically died with him. He never established himself as an artist because he never committed to the hard work of making it happen. It was not talent that he lacked but rather effort. As a result, he never accomplished his dream.

Yes, achieving our goal—reinventing our life—requires action.

Like the first artist I mentioned, some people who want to be writers commit to writing a certain number of words every day. This is the type of person who becomes a writer. If a person writes a thousand words a day for an entire year, he or she will produce 365,000 words—enough words for several novels or hundreds or even thousands of poems. Whether these poems or novels are published or not, I think you'll agree that such a person is a writer. And if that person writes this amount of words every day all year long, he or she will probably develop a habit that will enable the completion of several books every year. This habit is what makes the person a writer. In fact, whether the person who paints every day, writes every day, or fixes engines every day is financially successful yet or not, he or she is *already* an artist, writer, or mechanic. The person has already become that role. Achieving financial and popular success is another step.

We can't simply decide to become a singer and expect to wake up the next morning a superstar.

You've probably heard successful people joking that it took them thirty years of work in their profession to become "an overnight success." Action is required. And although the work toward our personally chosen goal might be easier and more joyful once we've decided what we want, it is still work, and there will still be difficult times—times when we might be tempted to give up.

In many ways, reinventing ourselves is like being a farmer or tending a garden. We decide what we want to plant, prepare the land, put in the seeds, work to keep the land in good shape, patiently wait for the rain, fight back the weeds and locusts, and then wait for the crops or flowers to spring forth. It is a process, and it takes planning and work to get to the joy at the end.

One of the best ways to ensure success is to keep striving consistently toward our goals—to develop the habit of regularly moving forward toward them. Like the artist who committed to painting *every day for one year* and the writers who committed to writing a thousand words *every day*, once we work consistently, our output will amaze us and spur us on.

To give ourselves more confidence in reinventing our life and make it easier to succeed, we can break the effort down into the following simple steps:

1. Want to change.
2. Analyze ourselves and our lives to understand who we are and what we want.
3. Make a decision about who we are and what we want.
4. Develop a plan or strategy to help us get there.
5. Develop habits, routines, systems, and processes that move us toward our larger goal and vision.
6. Actually do and be what we want to do and be.
7. Persist in our efforts to reach our goal of reinventing ourselves. Some people call this persistence *grit* and consider it one of the most essential factors in success.

■　■　■

Perhaps the most important thing about 1996 was that it was the year I put the pieces together as far as my "calling," or life's mission, was concerned.

Over the years, I had begun to realize that, even though I had lost my leg and suffered from a poor self-image and low self-esteem, I was more positive than many of the people I knew. Imagine how miserable they were feeling!

I had also begun to believe that maybe I could do something to help defeat the very things that had tried to destroy me—low self-esteem, poor body image, losing my dream, feeling like a failure in my love life, and drifting along without a firm mission.

About that time, people often noticed that I was moving forward in my life—getting jobs, moving around the country, and pursuing my education—and without even trying, I found myself being asked by organizations, especially nonprofits, to give career workshops.

As a result, I founded a company called Dream Reach Win, Inc., to motivate and empower individuals to conquer their personal limitations (real and perceived) and achieve their vision of success. For years, I had struggled against various types of difficulties, and now I wanted to share with others how to live and thrive in the face of adversity. I had learned that self-determination, self-love, courage, hard work, persistence, and faith are the essential ingredients to make one's life powerful. I also knew from my own life experiences that attitudinal barriers that exist in our society and inside ourselves can be obstacles to success, especially for people with disabilities. I believed that my courageous attitude and spirit could serve as a living testament to those who wanted to really live life and not just survive it!

For years, using the classroom as my stage, I had enlivened, inspired, and motivated my students with my personal testimony, life-skill strategies, interactive instructional activities, humor, and action-oriented techniques. Now, I wanted to take it to a higher level. Over time, I developed a variety of presentations on such topics as diversity in the workplace, middle-age adults in career transition, and career exploration for adolescents.

30

My Search for Meaning

"Throw yourself into some work you be-lieve in with all your heart. Live for it ... and you will find happiness that you had thought could never be yours."

—DALE CARNEGIE

I had discovered "my meaning in life," and I was on fire.

In his book *Man's Search for Meaning*, Dr. Viktor E. Frankl, a psychiatrist, neurologist, and survivor of the Nazi concentration and extermination camps during the Holocaust, explains how essential it was to their survival for people in the concentration camps to have meaning in their lives. He argues that "man's search for meaning is the primary motivation in his life. ... This meaning is unique and specific in that it must and can be fulfilled by him alone. ..."

Frankl's work also provides an explanation for the way I had been dealing with life after my cancer diagnosis and amputation. He explains how those who were confined in concentration camps for an indeterminate period of time and didn't know when or if they would ever get out were often not able to develop an ultimate goal and therefore stopped living for the future.

This was how I had experienced life for so many years—living in fear that the cancer would return and claim my life, afraid that I would have no future. As a result, perhaps subconsciously, I believed that having and striving for a "real" goal was useless.

The important thing was not that I found *the* meaning of life but rather that I found meaning in *my* life—unique and specific meaning in something that must and could be fulfilled by me alone. The combination of our talents, skills, desires, and background makes us unique and uniquely qualified for our purpose. Only I could accomplish Dream Reach Win and what it intended to do because of my unique combination of life experiences. It was my responsibility to fulfill Dream Reach Win's mission now, and knowing that gave me the strength to work harder for it, even as I was still dealing with the adversity in my life.

As the philosopher Friedrich Wilhelm Nietzsche said, "He who has a why to live can bear almost any how." I now had my reason, *my why*, and I knew that I could deal with any outward circumstances.

Satisfaction in our life comes from agreement between our internal self and our external self, both working in unison for the common good. To achieve such satisfaction and to maintain it, we need to regularly evaluate and examine ourselves and how we relate to our family, community, and the world to ensure that we are living according to our chosen purpose. One way to assess whether we are succeeding in this is to think about what we would want others to say about us after we die. We need to regularly ask ourselves these questions:

- What do I want my obituary to say?
- Am I living in a way that would lead to that obituary?
- Who am I?
- Who and what do I want to be?
- Do I matter?
- What is my place and purpose in life?

For me, fighting and surviving cancer at an early age forced me to start confronting such serious questions at a time when I would have much preferred to be dating and dancing at a disco somewhere. It took me a long time to answer them, but I ultimately realized that my purpose needed to be driven by God's purpose. And I still believe that today.

Over the decades, I partially reinvented myself many times as my vision of who and what I wanted to be changed or became clearer. Sometimes, even though I was doing well and was successful in other people's eyes, I realized that I wanted something else for my life.

People were often surprised when I left good, well-paying jobs that had great opportunities for advancement to take lower-paying jobs or return to college and live like a student again.

For some reason, I think I must have known that success for an individual is truly only success if it is *his or her version of success*.

I am glad that we live in a time when such reinvention is often possible. Even if we have a degree in law, engineering, or medicine, we can decide to do something else, perhaps open a small shop or restaurant or studio. Many people have done just that. And even if we've changed our careers or relationships or purpose many times already, we can symbolically lift up that clay pot that is our life, cast it to the ground, and watch it shatter into thousands of pieces. We can then analyze it, dream of a new picture for what our life should be, and start to work making that new mosaic—that new, reinvented life.

31

Thank You, God, for Saving Me

"And the day came when the risk to remain tight in a bud was more painful than the risk it took to blossom."

—ANAIS NIN

"Donna," my doctor said during my 1997 cancer checkup, "why are you still coming here every year? You've been cancer-free for twenty-one years. You have done remarkably well and have far surpassed the five-year expected survival rate. There's only a very low risk that the bone cancer will return after so long."

I was silent, and he laughed a little.

"You know," he said, "your chance of being killed by a jealous woman is greater than your chance of being killed by cancer."

What made the doctor say this? From 1997 until now, I sometimes find myself haunted by those words.

Over my years of going for annual checkups, I had matured and was coming into myself as a confident, beautiful, and quite fashionable young woman, and men—and their girlfriends—were taking notice.

"Your achievements and good looks transcend your amputation, and many women will wish they have what you have," the doctor continued. "They will want to be like you."

While I appreciated the boost to my self-esteem, I still don't understand why I might have to die at the hands of a jealous woman one day. Nevertheless, it has been more than forty years since my amputation now, and I still remain cancer-free.

I think that my doctor's point that the cancer was unlikely to return was very important for me on a subconscious level. It allowed me to believe that I had a great chance of living and that I was free to dream with abandon.

It also reminds me to be constantly on the lookout for jealous women—just in case!

32

The Power of Our Thoughts

"Our thoughts are either a fierce army of enemies marching to destroy us or compassionate paramedics coming to our rescue."

—Donna R. Walton

In 1997, I developed an interest in cognitive behavioral therapy while I was working at the Salvation Army Rehabilitation Program where I taught life skills classes to ex-offenders and substance abusers. To learn more about this area of psychology, I read several scholarly books and self-help books by Albert Ellis, Dr. Wayne W. Dyer, and Deepak Chopra.

This search helped me better understand why I became depressed when my self-esteem was under attack, why I needed to work so hard to build and maintain positive self-esteem, and how to improve my life by controlling my thoughts.

As a result, I began structuring my classes so that my students could also see and benefit from understanding the connection between their thoughts and their behavior.

Around this time, I was also awakened by a professor's research, which found a positive relationship between self-concept and adjustment to disability, regardless of age, disability, or other characteristics of the samples.

A combination of these things ultimately led me to pursue becoming a certified cognitive behavioral therapist through the American College of Certified Forensic Counselors (ACCFC), which is the Certification Commission of the National Association of Forensic Counselors.

While I benefited from writing down my feelings in a journal and reading scholarly and self-help books, I also got the opportunity to benefit from professional therapy in 1999 as a requirement for my doctoral degree. This requirement was based on the idea that good counselors get therapy too—that the only way to help others is to help yourself first.

Still, since I had gotten my life together to some extent over the previous years, I balked a little at the idea of participating in therapy at that time.

▓ ▓ ▓

As I sat in my car outside the therapist's office before my first session, I wondered why I was there—other than to fulfill my degree requirements.

I was nervous.

In retrospect, it's kind of funny. Even though I was studying to be a cognitive behavioral therapist, I still had the stereotypical concerns about therapy.

Did seeking therapy mean that a person couldn't cope with life, had mental problems, was weak?

Finally, I got up the courage and went inside the building, telling myself that if professional therapy was fine for movie, music, and sports stars, it was also fine for me.

When I finally went inside the therapist's office, she smiled and held out her hand to greet me. "Please have a seat," she said in a very calming voice, as she directed me toward a comfortable sofa.

The session began just as I expected with the anticipated first question: "What brings you here?"

I soon found that talking about my confusion, self-esteem issues, fear, unsatisfying relationships, and other problems really made me feel better.

Although I only attended sessions for a little under a year, they were healing and brought me to a much better acceptance of my disability and how it affected my life. The therapy especially helped me understand how my disability and I would have to co-exist and get along if I was going to be the diva—the empowered woman—I wanted to be.

It was the best medicine for my soul and spirit that I could have given myself, and I'm glad now that I gave it a chance.

One of the things my personal reading, my doctoral education, and my therapy sessions taught me was how much our thoughts impact us. I now know that one of the reasons it took me a long time to reinvent myself after my cancer diagnosis and amputation was that I, like many (probably even most) people, was guided by irrational thinking.

Such irrational thinking can include things like too much negative thinking and pessimism, too little positive thinking and optimism, catastrophizing (or always expecting the worst to happen), and overgeneralizing things (for example, thinking that *everything* is screwed up because a few things are going wrong or that *no one* will ever love us because a few people have rejected us). I learned that to be resilient and succeed, I needed to overcome these irrational thought habits.

When we spend too much of our thinking on the negatives and pessimism and too little on the positives and optimism, it can drain our energy and enthusiasm. It can make us feel like not even trying because "What's the point?"

Catastrophizing is even more extreme. If we expect that the worst is going to happen, we become fearful of the future. For me, I had always feared that the cancer would return and take my life, and perhaps that had held me back from pursuing the life I really wanted. Why try so hard if I was going to die from cancer soon anyway, right?

Overgeneralizing is when we take something and consider it all-inclusive and without exceptions. Our irrational overgeneralizing can usually be recognized by our use of words like *always*, *never*, *everyone*, *no one*, *everybody*, *nobody*, *all*, *none*, *everything*, *nothing*, and so on.

"*Nothing* good ever happens to me!"

"*Nobody* cares about me!"

"*Everybody* thinks I'm ugly (or stupid or worthless or untalented, etc.)!"

"I'll *never* succeed!"

"I'll *always* be a failure!"

Unfortunately, as humans, we tend to see things as either black or white when, in reality, things tend to be gray. When our day has not gone well, we say, "This is the *worst* day of my life. It *absolutely* sucks," forgetting that we are still alive, had three delicious meals, were able to take a nap, and got hugs from our children when we got home. We allowed the many good things we experienced in the day to be overshadowed by the three bad hours we experienced.

When we think or speak in absolutes, we are usually overgeneralizing, and we are usually wrong. There are almost always exceptions. Therefore, whenever we find ourselves using such all-inclusive language, we should reevaluate what we are saying and what we are believing. It could improve our feelings dramatically.

While my own thoughts had not been totally irrational over the years, they had been up and down, positive and negative. As a result, even with my naturally positive and upbeat personality and high self-esteem, I had experienced both "good" and "bad" periods in my life.

In relationships, I had come to believe that *nobody* would ever fully love me the way I wanted to be loved because I was "handicapped, disabled, crippled, flawed, less than a woman."

In thinking about my future, even many years after the cancer had been out of my life, I was catastrophizing and thinking that it would return and take my life, and this had perhaps held me back from pursuing a full life of hope and dreams and fulfilling my true purpose. And without the purpose that a person needs to truly live, I was not fulfilling my destiny, not being who and what I was meant to be.

Once I started breaking the shackles of irrationality that were binding me, however, my life began to improve dramatically.

By the time I'd entered my doctoral program in rehabilitation counseling and had begun participating in therapy, I had already changed a lot of my thinking and had begun fixing myself. However, the understanding I gained from my training and therapy helped me develop and heal even further. I now had a better understanding of the problems I had dealt with and, in some cases, had actually caused myself.

I also realized that even if a person is normally rational and positive, it only takes a small dose of irrationality and negativity to ruin it. It's like the old saying about one bad apple spoiling the bunch. Irrationality and negativity must, therefore, be beaten down as soon as they rear their ugly heads. We must immediately defeat them through rational thoughts, positive self-talk, and affirmations. The battle of thoughts is truly a battle for who and what we are.

> *"You have power over your mind—not outside events. Realize this, and you will find strength. The happiness of your life depends upon the quality of your thoughts."*
>
> —Marcus Aurelius

Of course, all of this is not as easy as it sounds. It doesn't just work automatically when we read that we must change and monitor our thoughts. Often these negative, highly destructive thoughts are deeply rooted habits and have become a part of what each of us sees as "my story." It is therefore important to realize that solving the problem might take time. Positive, rational thinking must also become a habit.

I was tired of having low self-esteem and a poor self-image, but to rebuild them, I had to realize that I was not going to get them back from a new prosthesis, the miraculous regrowth of my lost limb, or from another external source. It wasn't going to come from convincing everyone to stop being cruel. It would rather have to come from within myself—from taking the focus off my missing limb and putting it on the many things I had left. It would come from recognizing that I am much more than the sum of my physical parts and am also defined by my feelings, thoughts, beliefs, ideas, relationships, talents, abilities, and many other things. I would have to continually affirm my positive qualities and characteristics and silence or ignore the negative voices from inside and outside myself.

As I built up my self-esteem and self-image, I also knew that I would have to maintain them as other people reminded me of my missing limb, past failures, and current problems and as my own inner judge, or critic, tried to bring me down from within.

My doctoral studies and therapy instilled more deeply in me the understanding that I needed to focus not on the external things that I could not control or change—my missing limb, other people's feelings toward me, and other people's prejudices—and instead focus more on the things I could control and change… especially my own thoughts and perceptions.

While I had already understood this at some level as evidenced by the letter I'd sent myself in 1996, the reiteration of this concept and a more research-based understanding of it helped me implement it more fully.

33

The Wind Beneath My Wings

After the year 2000, I really began to soar. I knew now that my purpose was to teach others that they could thrive even when their circumstances seemed to indicate otherwise.

Even though many things were starting to improve for me, being back in college was tough, especially because of my limb loss. Over the years since my amputation, I have spent a lot of years on college campuses, and I can say without hesitation that they can be difficult places for people with disabilities.

While I always wanted to "be normal," to fit in with my peers, instead I was usually thought of, and sometimes referred to, as "the girl with the handicap." Because I used crutches in the early stages of my undergraduate experience before graduating to a cane, I was self-conscious and avoided participating in events that would put me out in public. I began to withdraw from the public that I had once craved.

On every level, from undergraduate through graduate school, being an amputee who used crutches or a cane and who limped was a significant obstacle. It was daunting to be among younger students without disabilities who seemed to have it so much easier on campus than I did.

At the time, I tried to hide or minimize my disability as much as possible.

Even when I was a doctoral candidate at The George Washington University, accessibility was still an issue. Something as simple as parking was often a significant obstacle for me. If I wanted a parking space close to class, I needed to pay an exorbitant amount of money for a permit, and while I was a student, that was not economically feasible for me.

I often had to go to campus an hour early to wait for a parking space to open up near my building. Then, as I sat in class with my fellow students later in the day, my energy and enthusiasm were often already drained by the obstacles I had to overcome just to get there. And that was on a good day. When the weather was difficult—especially when there was rain, snow, or ice—I would already be worn out before the first class began—if I was able to make it to the class at all.

In addition to parking problems and problems walking in inclement weather, I also had days when my residual limb was swollen and would not fit in my prosthesis without pain or at all.

There were other times when I was distracted from my work by phantom pain or back pain caused by my amputation and the use of a prosthesis. Unfortunately, because these various types of pain were invisible to others, they were often neither acknowledged nor respected.

In time, I would learn to demand respect, but it was fairly late by then. I should have demanded respect earlier, during my undergraduate and master's degree years, but in those days, I just wanted to seem as "normal" as possible and not stand out any more than I already did. I was uncomfortable putting myself out there any more than I had to, and as a result, I often suffered in silence.

It was during my doctoral studies, however, that I began to change.

I knew that many of the institutional barriers on campus were merely physical manifestations of a lack of awareness and a lack of internal systems to accommodate individuals with disabilities. So during this period, even though I knew that people were often uncomfortable talking about disabilities, I began to educate and intentionally create dialogue about my disability to help create awareness and understanding.

Even if it was uncomfortable for me and those I talked to, it was far better than students with disabilities having to endure additional hardships. In my opinion, it was definitely time for a change.

■ ■ ■

In 2000, while I was director of vocational services at the Whitman-Walker Clinic (now Whitman-Walker Health) in DC, I started a program called GO (Greater Opportunities) Now, which was an employment service that helped clients affected by HIV/AIDS acquire the skills and confidence they needed to seek and gain employment. The program also trained employers on the civil rights laws that foster equal employment opportunities for people with disabilities.

Then in August 2002, although I still hadn't completed my doctorate, I was hired as a faculty member at The George Washington University teaching graduate-level rehabilitation counseling courses using a distance-education format. This position helped me accelerate my progress, complete more coursework, and work on my dissertation.

In August 2005, as I stood on the stage to receive my doctorate degree in counseling, I looked out into the large audience of family, friends, and other spectators and felt that I was embarking on a new and exciting journey.

It had taken me nearly ten years and a lot of hard work to achieve this great accomplishment, and I was proud to have not given up. Of course, there had been times when I felt like it, but my determination had carried me through.

I was actually the first person in my immediate family to earn a doctorate, so it was especially gratifying. My closest friends showed their happiness for my accomplishment, but the deepest and proudest expressions were from my parents, who both sat in a very cozy office where I defended my dissertation and were given the news along with me that I had passed my defense.

"I am so proud of you, baby," Dad said. "You really know your stuff."

I didn't know at that time how much this degree would impact my life, but I know now that it has made a huge difference in how I am perceived and was an essential part of reinventing myself as an educator.

I strongly agree with Malcolm X, who said, "Education is the passport to the future, for tomorrow belongs to those who prepare for it today." With my doctorate in hand, even though I am black, female, and disabled, I have what I need to successfully navigate the often-challenging job-seeking terrain. I am now a much more valuable candidate for potential employers, and I have far less competition for positions because usually only a few candidates possess the required qualifications. As planned, my doctorate also gives me more credibility when I speak to others and interact with them on behalf of my organizations. "Dr. Walton" has proved to be a much more impactful title than "Ms. Walton."

34

There Will Be Glitches

All of this does not, of course, mean that the obstacles in my life disappeared. The struggle to achieve life satisfaction is constant, and the process of learning how to overcome difficulties does not end until death. Since life is all about change and challenges, our greatest challenge is learning to live our lives in the midst of such challenges.

Even after I discovered the life I wanted to pursue, everything did not suddenly become smooth and easy. There are still glitches along the way today.

Such is life.

If we really want to reinvent ourselves, however, we must have the resilience to stick to our goals regardless of the obstacles.

Many individuals with disabilities have found ways to continue pursuing their dreams despite seemingly overwhelming difficulties. One tattoo artist lost his dominant arm to amputation and learned to produce tattoos with his other arm—no easy feat. Try drawing with your non-dominant hand sometime if you think it's easy. Others with disabilities have learned to draw or paint with their mouth, and some musicians who have no arms have learned to play instruments with their feet. Richard Hopley, a poet who has cerebral palsy, wrote an entire book by typing on an iPad with his nose.

A young woman I'll call Annie earns her living as a writer and editor. A few years ago, however, she began having severe pain in her hand, wrist, arm, and shoulders and has found it difficult to use her computer. She still has the need—even the compulsion—to write, however, and she has tried to find ways to overcome her pain so that she can work. She sometimes writes in longhand; sometimes types on a small iPod with her thumbs, which is easier on her but still causes pain; and has invested in software that inputs her spoken words as text. She still has to use her computer too, though, and sometimes suffers excruciating pain from it, yet she finds solutions to continue working.

It's difficult, I know, but it's almost always possible to find a way to do something if you don't give up.

Even people who are considered great successes in their lives and careers have faced obstacles along their paths. Although it might look as if it was easy for them, famous people like J.K. Rowling, Oprah Winfrey, and Muhammad Ali struggled to achieve success.

Steve Jobs was actually pushed out of Apple in 1985 when he was 30, many years after he had worked so hard to turn it into a billion-dollar company.

Talk about a glitch!

But that's not the end of the story—not by a long shot.

In 1996, a struggling Apple sought Jobs out and brought him back to become CEO in 1997. And—with the development of the iPod, iPad, and iPhone under his leadership—the rest is history.

Unfortunately, even after we've begun rebuilding our lives and redefining ourselves—even after we've found our purpose and have come a long way on our chosen path—it is still possible that we will from time to time be pushed or pulled back into our old ways of thinking.

Years ago, long after I'd regained my positive self-image and self-esteem, I began to want to reach "normalcy," which I used to define as "walking without a limp." The fact was that I still didn't want to be perceived as an amputee in my daily life.

Because my residual limb is so short, it doesn't give me a long enough lever to control a prosthesis well, so I still limped after all of those years. I began to think about advanced technology and to dream again of having an artificial leg that would enable me to walk without a limp; I just wanted to be me, not the object of everyone's curiosity.

It's not unusual for people with disabilities to have such dreams of being what the world considers "normal," but I thought that I was past that. Unfortunately, in thinking like this again, I almost risked losing the positive self-image and high self-esteem I'd worked so hard to build and maintain over the years—all because I thought I had to walk "normally" again to attain society's ideal of physical attractiveness.

I was extremely excited when I had the opportunity to get a new four-bar pneumatic knee—the knee unit of choice for many above-knee amputees. I thought that this new knee would help me better hide the fact that I am an amputee from the rest of the world.

Oh, but what an experience it turned out to be! You see, I had this fantasy that this leg would transform my gait from a limp to a saunter. I was so excited that I was graduating to a high-tech leg that would allow me to walk without a limp and without a cane.

Unfortunately, I quickly became very disappointed and frustrated with the new knee.

I had been so caught up in the dream of walking smoothly, swiftly, and without a limp that I didn't realize the challenges that I would have to deal with, such as the weight of the knee and the limitations inherent in having such a short residual limb. My prosthetists probably knew that I might not realize my dream of walking without a limp, but they dared not tell me for fear of killing my fantasies.

I really wanted to be fitted with a computerized leg, but it wasn't an option because my insurance would not pay for it, and I wasn't financially prepared to pay for one on my own. Such legs can cost more than $32,000—a very high price indeed to pay for "normalcy."

My difficulty in walking with my new four-bar pneumatic knee was highly frustrating and caused me to have bouts of insecurity. I ultimately had to face the fact that I wasn't going to be able to function any better with it.

Fortunately, I was able to realize that giving up on this new knee was not admitting defeat. Instead, I was simply changing my goal again. My quest for years had been to walk without a limp. I realized now, however, that my situation could have been much worse. I might not have been able to walk at all. So from 2006 until today, my quest is just to walk, with or without a limp. I realize now that there is a great value in that—and that the rest is extra.

I mean, why should amputees even care about what others think about their gait? Just being able to walk or to get where we want to go, whether it is with a cane or in a wheelchair, is the point, isn't it? When we strive to make others comfortable, we sometimes lose our focus on what really makes *us* comfortable. Today, I no longer strive for a perfect gait. I've come to terms with how I walk. I walk with a limp. I use a cane. And this is my normalcy. This is it, and I'm OK with that. My "gimpy gait" is mine, and it is very "normal" to me.

During this period, I learned or re-learned something very important: Not only should we not judge others based on the way they look or walk, but just as importantly, we should also not judge ourselves. As I mentioned previously, that inner judge and critic will keep trying to return over and over, and we must continually beat it back if we want to live a life of joy and success. It hates winners.

I still face that inner voice today sometimes when I read through magazines I receive for amputees and see advertisements for amazing new prosthetic legs. With the convergence of new technologies, it appears that there might soon be a day when artificial limbs will be so advanced that they are almost the same as the real thing—even including the ability to be controlled by thought alone and with prosthetic "skin" that can "feel."

We've come a long way since that first artificial leg I received in 1976.

As I said, I have come to accept my gait as it is, limp and all, but will this new technology ultimately seduce me into thinking I should get one of these new devices? Will it convince me to try to reinvent myself as a woman who walks so well that no one would know that she is an amputee—that she has a disability?

Hmmm. It's not something I would rule out. But if I do decide to try again, there will be a major difference: The effort this time will come from a place of strength, not one of weakness. It won't be because I think I have to walk without a limp. It'll be because I believe that there is no reason I shouldn't. It won't give me more value. It won't make me better. It will simply enhance my mobility and make my life easier.

35

From Dream Reach Win to LEGGTalk

In 2006, I upgraded Dream Reach Win and changed its name to LEGGTalk, Inc. In this business, I use my life experience, personal testimony, and professional training to offer "**L**essons of **E**mpowerment for Achieving **G**oals and **G**reatness." LEGGTalk's services currently include public speaking, life coaching/counseling, empowerment workshops, and disability awareness and training.

With my new life as a greater testament that individuals can achieve abundance with a positive spirit and attitude and the determination to soar, I travel around the country to educate and motivate others to change their thinking, attitudes, and behavior. I share my principles for achieving success and motivational messages with a range of audiences, including those at business conferences and conventions, corporate staff meetings, high-school commencements, health and wellness events, universities, and other venues. Over the years, I have made motivational presentations at The National Council of Negro Women, Federally Employed Women (FEW), the Annual Conference on Disabilities, Ball State University, and many other events and places. I work with individuals, corporations, government agencies, hospitals, prosthetic and orthotic clinics, support groups, nonprofit organizations, and many other types of institutions. Through these services, I teach people to use their inner power to become champions—people who strive to win, no matter what their circumstances.

In addition to my public speaking, I provide life coaching and counseling via one-on-one or group sessions with a focus on personal enrichment. I act as an empowerment coach, challenging clients to visualize success and strive for it. I help them set priorities, establish clear goals, create strategies, and design action plans that make sense for them and help them achieve large and small "wins." The frequency, format, and content of my coaching sessions are tailored to each client's needs.

I also offer workshops and training in career development. As I mentioned earlier, many people have been reported to have said, "If you don't know where you're going, you will probably end up somewhere else." Unfortunately, many people are already there. They've found that their career isn't progressing the way they dreamed—or it may not even be the career they want. I help such people plan their future so that they can advance their life, not just by going forward but by going forward on the path *they have chosen*.

I have also developed what I call Empowerment Salons for women with and without disabilities. In these Empowerment Salons, I help women recognize and isolate the areas that block their growth in both their professional and personal lives. These interactive workshops offer self-empowerment training and are designed to help individuals overcome fears, build assertiveness skills and self-confidence, and embrace their inner spirit. A typical Empowerment Salon explores some of the most critical barriers to success and provides strategies to address them. Participants and I discuss self-esteem and how to get it back and keep it. We also discuss such topics as body image, beauty, how to dress, and whether or not we are putting our best self in front of others. Other potential barriers include fear of failure or success, fear of rejection, procrastination, disorganization, poor decision-making, and poor or no planning.

I share my story and how I went within to find the beauty inside me and then was able to reflect it on the outside by always dressing well and smiling a lot to always present myself in an attractive way. We also talk about what our behaviors might look like when we don't have high self-esteem. While I was promiscuous and did not choose great partners, others might drink, do drugs, or allow themselves to be abused, as we each reflect our low self-esteem in different ways.

Just as some women choose to frequent beauty salons to have their nails manicured, hair coiffed, or eyebrows waxed, others may choose to attend my Empowerment Salons to develop assertion skills, build their self-confidence, learn about establishing and maintaining relationships, get motivated, and even learn how to budget. The topics covered might include goal setting and action planning; dealing with adversity; improving effective communication; advocacy; health and wellness; and spirituality.

Because research has shown over and over the important connection between mind, body, and spirit and how, when all three of these elements are in sync, we can accomplish almost anything, I strive to include all three of these elements in our discussions.

These sessions may also be conducted in the form of brown-bag lunch sessions called Empowerment Lunch Box Just4U and customized for the workplace to teach employees ways to live and work passionately in the face of stress, adversity, and other obstacles.

Also, believing strongly in the power of personal testimony, I have written articles for national publications that uncover social prejudice and attitudinal bias and that help young girls and women with disabilities confront their challenges and believe in themselves.

My disability awareness and training workshops focus on bridging barriers between individuals with and individuals without disabilities by exploring negative attitudes and behaviors that undermine service to people with disabilities in workplace environments. We work with corporations, nonprofit organizations, and government agencies that serve individuals with disabilities, including bus and paratransit agencies and educational institutions. The workshops emphasize disability awareness, sensitivity training, workplace guidelines for accommodating people with disabilities, and disability-competency training for classroom instructors, school counselors, and others.

As a result of my management experience in vocational rehabilitation and system change, I have made a direct impact on job development and job placement for individuals with disabilities. In fact, my leadership in this area has led to an increase in the hiring of people with severe disabilities in both the public and private sectors. Furthermore, I have served as a public speaker at engagements to advocate on behalf of people with disabilities. In essence, I explain to employers and others the difference between being disabled and enabled. Moreover, I discuss the social and political reasons people with disabilities will always be necessary contributors to the workforce. My mission to champion the rights of people with disabilities is ongoing.

> *"I remember using terms such as* handicapped, confined to a wheelchair, *and* seeing-eye dog. *In a very nice way, Donna said, 'Mark, the proper names are* disability, wheelchair user, *and* service dog. *She is constantly teaching, whether it is through her job … or with friends. Teaching and informing people is in her blood."*

—MARK HARRIS, LONGTIME FRIEND

> *"Donna knew her life was spared to share her experience with the world, to help others like her, and to engage in the advancements of the laws, medical standards, etc., for the disabled."*

—VANDA PAYTON, LONGTIME FRIEND

36

My Mosaic

So after many years of striving to reinvent myself into who and what I wanted to be, what was the result? The following is my description of the mosaic I produced:

I am Bold,
Brilliant,
Courageous,
and Fabulous too.

I am Powerful
and at times Provocative,
Creative,
Caring, and Compassionate.

I am an Advocate,
an Educator,
a Motivator.

And I also happen to be a person with a disability.

And while the word "disability" may apply to me, it does not define me.
Because I am more than just the sum of my body parts.

This reinvention was on both a professional and personal level.

Although I was still interested in a romantic relationship, following my reinvention, I approached the possibility of finding love differently. Before, if I found someone attractive, I spent many hours obsessing over whether the person would reject me because of my cane and limp before getting to know me. It took effort and sometimes lots of it, especially since I believed many men might consider me "less of a woman." The amount of energy that I put into this kind of thinking was exhausting and to a great extent unrepresentative of the type of person I truly am—bold and confident.

Now if I see someone I'm attracted to, I'm more comfortable in who I am. If he likes me, great. If not, it's all good. I have learned to respect other people's decisions, even if they do not include me. I'm not going to try to make somebody like (or love) me anymore. Either we click or we don't.

I know now that I also have something to offer in a relationship. If the other person wants it, we might work out. If not, as the old cliché says, "There are many more fish in the sea."

Now that I have reinvented who and what I am, I don't want others to have to unnecessarily spend the inordinate amount of time and effort I spent doing so. While I needed to go through some of the difficulties on my own to reach this point, many of the things I went through could have been avoided. I now want to help others avoid the slow and difficult process of re-invention and help them fast-track their development so they can become who and what they want to be as quickly as possible. In doing so, they can begin living their dreams now, not twenty or thirty years from now.

One of my main problems was that I was largely going through my reinvention alone and was moving forward simply by stumbling onto solutions from time to time. I didn't have a mentor to help me with my problems related to my disability, finding my true calling, and then developing and building my dream life and organizations. It's not necessary for others to go through this process so haphazardly, however. Although everybody's situation is different and there is no single road map for success, there are principles that I found and that I discovered on my own that can help others find their purpose and deconstruct and reconstruct their lives. Seeing this type of transformation in people and watching them accomplish things they never thought they could is a joy for me!

One of the things that concerns me most from my experience is how someone as confident and as positive as I am by nature—someone with naturally high self-esteem and who was born as emotionally strong and able to endure pain and stress as I am—could be brought so low by my situation and by other people's opinions and negativity.

If someone like me could be brought down by these things, what about those who are not as confident, as positive, and as strong and who are already experiencing low self-esteem before they face trials? Their chances of regrouping and overcoming such challenges are much lower than mine, and I fear for how damaged they might be.

That's why I'm committed to helping such people overcome all types of hurdles in their lives. If people can't live their dreams because of internal barriers, they already have invisible disabilities, perhaps in addition to visible ones.

37

Working Day and Night

"We are at our very best, and we are happiest, when we are fully engaged in work we enjoy on the journey toward the goal we've established for ourselves. ... It makes everything else in life so wonderful, so worthwhile."

—Earl Nightingale

At the time of this writing, in addition to running my business, I also work full-time to ensure that employees with disabilities are accommodated in the workplace. This work is in close alignment with the aspirations of my reinvented self, one of which is to help others with disabilities.

Some days as I work in my office, dealing with complaints from people with disabilities who are being discriminated against, I think about how far we have come in eradicating some discriminatory attitudes and actions and also how far we still have to go.

When I think about the discriminatory beliefs and practices I see today, I sometimes recall my own experiences. One experience especially stands out in that it shows how such harmful beliefs are formed early.

Back in 1981 when I was teaching a class in elementary school, a 7-year-old student spoke up.

"Miss Walton, you will never get married," he said.

"Why do you say that?" I asked.

"No man will ever marry a woman with one leg," he answered politely, as if his analysis were obvious.

I was fairly new at being an amputee and at teaching, and I stood before my class in silence, not knowing how to respond.

I did not know at the time what profound meaning this student's comment would have to the work I am doing today regarding diversity. I realize now that this student's value system and view of people with disabilities as "less" was shaped very early. I also know that some people with such beliefs have grown up to be business owners and managers of government agencies, companies, and hotels and still have the belief that people with disabilities are less competent, less skilled, and less capable. I sometimes wonder if generations of people might still be infected with such ideas.

Today, as a I work for equality in the workplace, I sometimes think of this student and realize that it will take a lot of education to change people's perceptions of people with disabilities—perceptions that have been taught and reinforced over centuries.

It is often difficult to fight this battle again and again when I believe that people should naturally consider equality the right thing. I wonder how any other opinion could have ever arisen and taken hold. Still, regardless of how these beliefs came about, they must be constantly countered, and I am proud that it is both my career and calling to do so.

38

The Divas Movement

"Yes!" I said out loud to myself. "This is absolutely awesome!"

I had launched a Facebook group page called "Divas With Disabilities" in December 2012 because I wanted to show that "diva" and "disability" can go together in a single person. With Divas, I wanted to reach out especially to women of color because of my own experiences as an African American woman.

I'd started the page simply as a way to connect and network with others and maybe make a few new friends. I had no idea or expectation that it would grow into anything else. But when I opened the page that day, I found a lot of activity and realized that perhaps the page was filling a need. Many women and the men who supported them had begun commenting and posting articles and resources on the page. In addition, my personal "experience as an amputee" postings especially seemed to be making an impact. Many visitors to the page said that they found refuge and inspiration in realizing they were not alone.

Over the coming months, the activity continued to grow, and I began to think of Divas With Disabilities as something much greater than I'd originally envisioned. I started posting to the page more often and then decided to expand and build a website for the project as well.

Today, the project is evolving into a major movement for women of color with all types of disabilities, and I'm consistently amazed at its increasing popularity.

Starting with fewer than fifty members, the group now has close to two thousand active followers. Members share news articles, diva images, and upcoming events of their own organizations. From 2013 to 2014, we started to receive e-mails from divas who wanted to help out with the project. We also received thank-you messages from women around the world and inquiries from other organizations that wanted to partner with us.

Unfortunately, perceptions of women with disabilities are still too often rooted in stereotypes rather than in reality. We are more than just our canes, crutches, wheelchairs, prosthetic devices, and limps. We are mothers and daughters and sisters. We are sexual beings. We are scientists, political leaders, professors, athletes, actors, and pretty much anything else you can think of.

I sometimes like to use the spelling *DisAbilities* to emphasize our abilities rather than our disabilities. Even though I walk with a limp, I have passion, fashion, and style. That's the point of the name of the movement—to demystify the notion of women with disabilities and to deemphasize the disability. While women with disabilities are a lot further along than we were decades ago, as shown by the popularity of *Push Girls*, a reality television series that features the lives of four women with paralysis, we still have a long way to go.

For purposes of the divas with disabilities movement, a diva is defined as an empowered woman, and the project promotes and empowers women of color who have disabilities, chronic medical conditions, and congenital anomalies. It is bringing together women throughout the world who execute daily tasks without letting their disabilities stand in the way, and it is amplifying their voices. We like to use the phrase "Showing Up Unapologetically" a lot. In fact, many of us are strong, influential leaders within our communities.

Our goal now is to thrust more women of color with disabilities into the spotlight through media exposure—to shape the perspective of "what disability looks like." Our movement is growing, and we are now reaching thousands of women with disabilities worldwide.

Currently, we are putting in place a Global Divas Ambassadors program that will help the project continue to thrive, educate, inspire, and empower. As we move forward on exciting new initiatives, our mission is to serve as a platform for women to learn, share, and grow and to empower them to live fulfilling lives. Expect to see more from the project in the future, including a television show, a mentorship program, an awards ceremony, a conference, and the establishment of a foundation. Our work has just begun.

■ ■ ■

One of the featured divas on our website is an amazing woman named Apryl Michelle Brown. In 2004, Apryl received black-market silicone injections to enhance her butt size, but unfortunately, the procedure went terribly wrong. As a result, she lost parts of both her arms, both her legs, and parts of her butt cheeks.

When I first read about her in an article in *Essence* magazine, I felt that I had to know her and that she had to know me. I contacted her through Facebook, and she brought out something in me. When we spoke on the telephone, we both exploded with joy and love for each other. I was amazed to find that after such a devastating loss, she was still so positive and upbeat, even during those times when I suspected she might not have been having a great day.

She made the point that, while she and I have lost body parts, many people have amputated spirits, which is the true disability. As Al Pacino's character in the movie *Scent of a Woman* says, "There is no prosthetic for [an amputated spirit]."

Apryl and I felt like kindred spirits. We both know the power of God's miracles, having both survived the medical statistics that suggested we would not. We'd both suffered loss, but we felt whole when we spoke with each other. We talked about how others sought us out to help them deal with their amputated spirits and what we could do to help empower them.

Today, Apryl is a passionate humanitarian, helping others through motivational seminars and public speaking tours. Her messages often focus on self-esteem and "loving the skin you're in." Her losses have not destroyed her will to live or her determination to succeed spiritually, mentally, and physically.

Her confidence, strength, and power have greatly influenced me to keep going and never give up. She inspires me to "rock what I got." And just like a typical diva, she's got style.

While Apryl truly exemplifies what Divas With Disabilities is all about, for every Apryl, there are so many women of color with disabilities who are living with amputated spirits and who are knocked down over and over by life's difficulties. Through The Divas With Disabilities Project, I hope to help them stand back up and become the divas I know they can be.

When I first started the Facebook group page that would later become The Divas With Disabilities Project, I was a little hesitant because I knew another project could add to the many daily tasks I already needed to perform.

I was, therefore, thrilled when I arranged to meet my friend Gail for dinner one evening in 2012 and she invited a young woman she'd supervised for an internship to join us. Her name was Erica Butler.

Erica's career goal was to work in TV journalism, and since that had been one of my aspirations, I was excited to talk with her about it. Likewise, she became excited when I told her about my Facebook group for women with disabilities. At that time, I believe that I was simply calling it Women With Disabilities. Erica is the one who suggested that I call the group Divas With Disabilities—a name that I immediately loved.

Erica later said the following about Divas With Disabilities and me:

This project has meaning. When the leader of any project can relate to its followers and supporters, the message drives home. Dr. Donna Walton has a disability just like many of her supporters and followers. She's passionate, and the women engaging on social media networks are passionate too. Witnessing this kind of eagerness is contagious. Someone without a disability could easily become attracted to such a dynamic group of women (including myself). ... Working with this project as the leading brand/communications consultant has driven me to develop my own business, EB Media Group. Dr. Walton is an incredible mentor and woman.

Although Erica is many years younger than I am, she is beacon of light for me because she believes as strongly in my work and my success as I do.

39

Keeping the Passion Alive

"A person can succeed at almost anything for which they have unlimited enthusiasm."

—CHARLES M. SCHWAB

As Steve Jobs said, it's essential to have passion for what you do because continuing to do it over a long period can be so difficult. "If you don't love it, if you're not having fun doing it," he said, "you're gonna give up."

■ ■ ■

I love what I'm doing—my calling—I told myself, but sometimes it's hard work, and I get tired.

I'd had a hard day at my full-time job, and when I got home, I was exhausted. I didn't just feel as if I were on a treadmill; I felt as if I were on about ten treadmills.

In addition to my full-time career, I need to maintain my organizations' websites and Facebook accounts, and I need to give speeches from time to time, lead seminars, be the spokesperson at conferences, and so on.

I knew I needed to put in some work to support LEGGTalk or Divas With Disabilities or my public speaking goals, but I just didn't have the energy. In fact, all I wanted to do was rest and not think or say anything about disability.

I know that consistent efforts—even if they are small—move me forward. Unfortunately, even though I'm a pretty strong woman—I've even called myself "super bad" at times—I'm not Wonder Woman. I am only human, and I need to rest, sleep, and recuperate from time to time.

One of my problems over the years—the one that sometimes causes me that feeling that I'm on ten treadmills—is that I, like many organization builders, have too often tried to do everything myself. Fortunately, it's a problem that I'm now overcoming. I have finally come to realize that I am simply not trained or able to accomplish all that needs to be done to build my organizations and keep them relevant and successful. I now know that to build a strong organization, "it takes a village," as they say.

There are just too many things that need to be done to keep my organizations running. There's management, marketing, public relations, branding, writing, editing, photography, video production, graphic design, speaking, holding workshops, being interviewed, website building and maintenance, social media, grant writing, fundraising, counseling, and accounting. One person cannot be an expert in all of these areas, and I am not passionate about all of these roles anyway. To help solve this problem, I have begun hiring others to assist with some of these functions. This strategy has enabled me to focus on the things I am most passionate about, move at a faster pace toward fulfilling my vision with more professionalism, and keep my passion for the organizations alive. Unfortunately, it can also be quite expensive.

The parts of "my calling" that I am most passionate about are the social outreach aspects and the opportunity to offer guidance to those who are seeking answers and/or validation. I love showing up and teaching spontaneously on a subject, such as looking beyond what is seen (the physical) and embracing the soul of a person. I also love public speaking and leading workshops and conferences.

I don't especially love all of the writing that I need to do, keeping up with social media, and marketing. If I had continued trying to do all of these things alone, I believe I would be burned out by now and might have even given up on my dreams.

I am still striving to achieve some other major goals, which are to host a national radio or television show and to be featured in a documentary about Divas With Disabilities. I have plans in place for achieving these passions, and I'll continue to seek out ways to keep these passions alive until I succeed.

The point is that even though I'm doing what I want to do, every aspect of it is not always fun and exciting. There are still times when it feels like I am working and struggling. That is normal, and I must make sure that these things alone do not discourage me.

I have found it essential to figure out which things I am most passionate about in my reinvented life and career and to ensure that I get some good opportunities to interact with those "passion spots," while also finding ways to avoid the "dreaded spots" as much as possible. Doing so helps me stay enthusiastic and keeps my dream from becoming simply another job.

Another way I've been able to keep my passion alive all of these years is simply by understanding that succeeding—fulfilling our dreams—takes work and time. I know what to expect so I can deal with the process and be patient.

When I realized that I wanted to make my new life about helping others reinvent their lives and fulfill their dreams, I soon realized that it wasn't just going to happen overnight. I was going to have to strive to make it happen. Although I have a strong desire and helping others achieve their dreams seems like a natural part of who I am, taking courses in college, getting my doctorate, and working in the field is what has made my dream a reality.

> *"I hated every minute of training, but I said, 'Don't quit. Suffer now and live the rest of your life as a champion.'"*

> —MUHAMMAD ALI

> *"It always seems impossible, until it's done."*

> —NELSON MANDELA

40

The Importance of Habits

"We are what we repeatedly do. Excellence, then, is not an act, but a habit."

—Aristotle

Habits are small goals that help us reach our larger goals. As such, they also help define who and what we are. Forming habits through consistent effort is one of the most important keys to changing our lives and fulfilling our purpose.

In pursuing my aspiration to always be defining who I am, developing certain habits has been essential. The following habits are supportive of my role as a businesswoman and public speaker:

- Practicing in front of a mirror before I present in front of an audience. If I don't practice, I stand a much larger chance of messing up—something a professional speaker can't afford to do too often. And I just don't need that kind of embarrassment anyway. Practicing before an event is a habit that has paid off over and over.

- Reading aloud to work on my voice. Just like my habit of brushing my teeth, I do this twice a day.
- Sitting in silence. I turn off all electronic devices every day for at least one hour to clear my mind.
- Meditating before going to bed so that I can relax and wake up refreshed and able to focus the following day.

I often share these strategies with my clients to show them how to establish their own "A Game" and put their best face forward. It is important that we understand that success is not the result of any one action. Instead, as author Robert Collier said, "Success is the sum of small efforts, repeated day in and day out."

Of course, developing and maintaining habits is not easy, but it is well worth the effort. As synchronized swimmer Sarah Bombell noted, "The pain of discipline is far less than the pain of regret."

41

What If I Don't Feel Like It?

Unfortunately, there are times when we just don't feel like doing anything, usually because we are exhausted from already having done too much, having allowed too many tasks to be put on our plate.

So what do I do to deal with such times in my own life or, even better, to prevent them?

Often when I get burned out or almost to that point, I do what I call "decompression," which requires emptying my mind of anything to do with disability and my organizations. Usually, this means napping and giving the creative chambers of my brain, which house my comedic side, a chance to play. I will think about characters, reflect on funny jokes that I've heard, or think about what I call "stupid television"—those programs that require only my laughter with no cerebral activity at all.

All of this comedic decompression will later come out in real life, and my friends are quite delighted by it. For me, it relieves a lot of stress that would probably otherwise negatively affect my health and my pursuit of my goals.

One of the ways I try to prevent getting burned out to begin with is to celebrate each time something good happens—whenever someone requests me to speak, teach a class, or serve on a work group, for example. Resoundingly proclaiming that I am "super bad," which for me is like being a superstar, I treat myself with great gifts, usually a unique piece of jewelry or clothing, dinner at a great restaurant, or a trip, such as the vacation I took in southern France a few years ago. My most recent big reward to myself was a brand new convertible sports car—a treat for surviving cancer for thirty-eight years! I know, such an extravagant *thirty-eight*-year anniversary gift seems a little unusual, but hey, I couldn't wait *forty* years. I wanted to celebrate the great gift of life now.

42

The Dreams Just Keep Coming True!

"Hold fast to dreams, for if dreams die, life is a broken bird that cannot fly."

—Langston Hughes

Sitting in the audience at the 40th Anniversary of the Rehabilitation Act at the Equal Employment Opportunity Commission (EEOC), I looked over and saw just the person I'd been wanting to talk to—Claudia Gordon. She is the first deaf black woman to have served in the White House Office of Public Engagement, which allowed her to be a liaison to the disability community and an adviser on disability policies. I'd been wanting to meet her for a while to tell her about The Divas With Disabilities Project, and there she was, presenting on a panel three rows away from me. Sometimes things just seem to happen in a way that benefits us, even though we've done no planning for them.

When I got the chance, I went over to her and introduced myself to the interpreter who would use sign language to help us converse. We chatted for a while, exchanged numbers, and said good-bye. I didn't know if I'd ever hear from her again.

A few weeks later, I received an e-mail from Claudia asking me if I'd like to participate in a conference call about the details of the White House National African American History Month celebration that would be held in February 2014 and my potential role in it.

Me? The White House? African American History Month? Celebration?

You can probably guess my answer.

"Absolutely," I said. "I'd love to participate."

So in 2014, I was officially tagged as an inaugural member of the White House Disability Liaison's Disability-African American Kitchen Cabinet and selected to serve as the moderator for a panel discussion during National African American History Month. This then led to my next invitation to the White House, serving as a subject matter expert on accessibility and inclusiveness for The White House Operations' Working Group.

Being invited to the White House was such a great recognition and validation of my work. When I was invited, I was both humbled and overjoyed. It was one more in a long line of proofs that hard work, even though it sometimes seems to be wasted, does ultimately come to fruition.

It was also more evidence that getting my doctoral degree was paying off. Were it not for my doctoral degree and my vast work experience, I do not believe I would have been selected to participate at the White House.

■　■　■

Although I was happy to see many of my dreams being achieved over the past several years, my dream of being a performer—of being in the spotlight—was still there. It was, therefore, especially gratifying in April 2014 when I received an e-mail from Wendy Crawford of the groundbreaking Raw Beauty NYC photography exhibit (www.therawbeautyproject. com), which showcases photographs of twenty women with various disabilities who represent beauty, sensuality, and empowerment. Wendy had discovered Divas With Disabilities through social media and invited me to be a model for the exhibit.

It was like coming back to my original dreams in a way. When I first lost my leg, I believed that my dream of being in the spotlight was over. And really, at that time it was true.

Fortunately, many people and organizations are now working to change that. Raw Beauty NYC, mobileWOMEN.org, Models of Diversity (www.modelsofdiversity.org), The Bold Beauty Project (www.boldbeautyproject.com), and my own organization, The Divas With Disabilities Project (www.divaswithdisabilities.com), are helping society realize that there is no single standard of beauty.

I grinned for a long time after reading Wendy's e-mail and sending one back to her agreeing to be a model for the project.

■ ■ ■

Beauty. Sensuality. Empowerment.

Just as planned, these three words were clearly in the minds of those walking through the Raw Beauty NYC exhibit as they gazed up at the photographs on the wall of twenty women with disabilities—including one of me.

As I wandered through the exhibit, I listened to the visitors' conversations and was glad to hear their positive responses to the photographs. I'd traveled to

New York from DC with my father and sister earlier in the day because I felt I had to be there for the opening. It was, after all, a victory for women in general, women with disabilities, and women of color—three groups I care deeply about.

Seeing these women—including me—up there on the wall in poses representing beauty, sensuality, and empowerment, I had to wonder why it had taken so long for people to realize that a disability is not *everything* about the person with a disability—that it is only a small detail. Regardless, my heart was dancing with joy.

The photographs were huge—maybe three feet by four feet—and were accompanied by a brief biography about each woman. Seeing all of those wonderful, inspiring women together up there, another word came to my mind: Astounding!

"The world breaks everyone and afterward many are strong at the broken places," Ernest Hemingway wrote in one of his novels. These photographs were graphic proof of this observation.

These "broken" women's lives also reminded me of the Japanese art of *kintsukuroi*, in which broken pots are put back together using lacquer mixed with powdered gold as an adhesive. Using this technique, the artist does not hide the "flaws" in the piece but rather illuminates them. Such pots, with jagged lines of gold running between the cracks, are considered more beautiful than the originals. These women—these beautiful, "broken" divas with disabilities—are, to me, living kintsukuroi works of art.

Still, regardless of their beauty, this type of exhibit could not have happened forty, thirty, twenty, or even ten years ago. The words *beauty*, *sensuality*, and *empowerment* would not have been used. People just weren't ready to see women with disabilities this way. The words used might have more likely been *handicapped*, *crippled*, *pitiful*, *weak*, *flawed*.

Later that night, after the exhibit opening, as my dad, my sister, and I headed back to our hotel in a cab beneath an illuminated Times Square sky, I felt like Cinderella being whisked away in a carriage. It was an amazing experience that I will never forget!

■　■　■

Shortly afterward, when things didn't seem as if they could get any better, more huge things happened in 2015.

An article about the Raw Beauty NYC Project was published in *O, The Oprah Magazine*, providing another opportunity to show others that life does not have to end because you lose a piece of you, you have a disability, or you look different from others.

It also gave me another chance to see myself as not only beautiful but as the celebrity I always dreamed of becoming.

While I'm glad to see the increased opportunities that are opening up for people with disabilities today, I realize that there's still a long way to go to overcome the stereotypes and stigma that go with disabilities and to achieve true equality.

Also, remember when my broadcasting dreams were crushed twice back in the '80s when I unsuccessfully interviewed for a broadcasting internship and unsuccessfully tried to get into the S.I. Newhouse School of Public Communications at Syracuse University? Well, more than three decades later, those dreams are back on! And as model, actress, musician, and singer Vanessa Williams said, "Success is the sweetest revenge."

▩　▩　▩

It's interesting how all of these wonderful opportunities and connections have come together from seeds I planted along the way and forgot about, not really expecting that they would end up bearing such fruit. My invitations to the White House, for example, grew out of my single chance meeting with Claudia Gordon at the 40th Anniversary of the Rehabilitation Act, and my invitation to host a radio show came from an interview I did about Divas With Disabilities.

Keeping this in mind, I am even more motivated than ever to continue assembling the broken pieces of my dreams and moving forward, to go on planting seeds even at times when little seems to be happening, because I never know how, when, or where those seeds will bear fruit.

There are no guarantees about the outcome of my efforts, but there are many examples of people who persisted toward the realization of their dreams for years until they ultimately saw them realized. I know it is possible because I am one of these people.

*"Whatever you do may seem insignificant,
but it is most important that you do it."*

—Mohandas Gandhi

43

We Fall Down, But We Get Up

*"It's not a sin to get knocked down; it's a sin
to stay down."*

—Carl Brashear

From the moment I woke up in the hospital after
my amputation until today, more than four decades later, I have never for more than a few minutes
or hours been able to forget about my missing leg.
From the time I awoke and saw the missing area under my blanket, this loss has been with me. For a long
time, when I was awake, I had questions about how I
was going to face my future, and when I was asleep, I
had nightmares about having one leg—perhaps trying
to escape a burning building with a missing leg, trying
to dance and not being able to, or a man reaching out
to touch me and finding nothing to touch.

If I had to wake up in the night to use the bathroom or make a sandwich, I had to put on my prosthesis or use my crutches or a wheelchair. My residual limb might itch or develop a blister. Others might ask me about my limp. I needed to schedule appointments with healthcare providers. I had to wear special shoes. I had to arrive early when I had appointments. I had to be careful in the rain or snow. And on and on. Whatever it was, there was always something to make me think of my missing leg. It was no longer there, but it was still my constant companion. Think about it. No one would ask me about my arms or the leg I still had. My missing leg got more attention than all my other body parts combined.

Losing a leg was not like losing a tooth or an appendix or having a tumor removed—things that might never be thought of again. It was permanently life affecting.

Nicholas John Vogt, a soldier who lost his legs in the war in Afghanistan, perhaps explained it best to David Jay, who interviewed him for *The Unknown Soldier* project. "The only thing that I want to pass on is this," Vogt said. "Losing limbs is like losing a good friend. We wish we could still be with them, but it wasn't 'in the cards.' Then we get up, remember the good times, and thank God for whatever we have left." (Reported by WBTV.com)

Probably the most important aspect of it to me was that it reinvented me and changed me from "Donna, the Star in Waiting," to "Poor Donna, the Handicapped, Disabled, Imperfect, Crippled, Flawed Girl."

What happened over the following four decades was me trying to reinvent myself, mostly subconsciously in the beginning and consciously later on.

I have felt like giving up many times. When I struggled to walk on campus with crutches. When I fell down in front of others. After chemotherapy treatments. When I was rejected by men or women or for jobs I deserved. So what prevented me from doing so?

For one thing, I believe that I simply do not have the DNA for giving up. I was always an achiever and always believed that I was destined for greatness in some way or another.

Fortunately, instead of turning to drugs or alcohol to cope with my pain, I kept going forward, even though I fell down from time to time.

Through self-analysis, prayer, hard work, and the planting of seeds, I ultimately reinvented myself again and again and threw away that Poor Donna identity that I had allowed others and my own inner critic to invent.

If we want to become who and what we want to be and achieve our dreams, we must believe that we can do so and never give up. I refused to quit, and as a result, I earned my bachelor's degree, master's degree, and doctoral degree against heavy odds. I have already achieved many of my dreams—some that I thought were completely lost—and I have many more that I'm still working on.

■　■　■

Ups and downs occur for all of us.

"Fall down seven times, get up eight," advises a Japanese proverb. Such simple but such profound advice.

We can often win simply by refusing to stay down, getting up just one more time than we fall. Nothing, it seems, can beat persistence, tenacity, outlasting the problem.

Although I went through some negative changes after my cancer and amputation, once I got back my positivity, I was able to get back to the core of me. When my survival gene was finally turned back on, I was like a caterpillar that became a butterfly.

As a result of dealing with my limb loss, the threat of death from cancer, and my experience living with a disability, I evolved so much as a person and no longer have the luxury of worrying or complaining about things that really don't matter in the grand scheme of things.

I thought that I'd lost everything when I lost my leg and my dream to be a performer. However, when I realized that my life was so much more than those two things, I was so thankful—thankful to still have one leg and, frankly, thankful to be alive.

Interestingly, it was losing my leg that led me to fulfill my destiny. I am certain that I would not be on the journey I'm on today were it not for losing my leg.

Like many people who have experienced great crises, I believe that loss can transform us into something better than we were before. Over the years, I have read the stories of numerous amputees—people who have lost one or all of their limbs—who say that amputation had a positive impact on their lives. After their amputation, they say, they became so much more than they were before. It made them appreciate their life and start living it more fully. Moreover, it changed them emotionally and helped transform them into better human beings.

I know it sounds unbelievable, but like many others, I believe that I've benefited much from the trauma in my life. I've learned a lot from it; in many ways, I've grown and improved.

When I think about my younger self—the know-it-all who really thought a little too much of herself and was probably a bit too proud—I wonder what that little girl might have become without a few strong doses of trauma and humility along the way. I'm glad that today, because of going through my own crises, I am thankful for everything I have and feel more empathy for others. As Ian MacLaren was reported to have said, we should "be kind, for everyone [we] meet is fighting a hard battle."

44

Shooting for the Moon

"Be the kind of woman that when your feet hit the floor every morning, the devil says, 'Oh, crap. She's up.'"

—U<small>NKNOWN</small>

After my amputation, people tended to treat me differently than they had before, which showed their limited expectations for my future. Ultimately, I rejected these limited expectations and decided that I would be much more than others imagined—that I would write my own success story.

In time, my strong sense of self and my absolute belief that God had a plan for me that did not include any kind of limited life was my salvation. Although I was certainly challenged by my new reality, the essential me had not gone anywhere. The diva was still there, although she was pushed down by periods of low self-esteem for many years.

Even though I ultimately came to terms with the fact that I was not going to be living the same life that I had before my amputation, I began fashioning a life that was still about *me*—she who would not be vanquished. This new picture I had in mind was not that of a victim but that of a powerful woman who would not merely survive, but thrive.

I wanted to affirm myself.

Myself. That part is important. I intended to show the world that I had the audacity to be what *I* wanted to be, not what *it* expected me to be.

Although it's a good idea to listen to other people's opinions and consider them when making decisions, in the end, we should not let them or our situation define us. When we are reinventing ourselves, we must do the defining.

Make no mistake; resolving to be a thriving, powerful woman was not a one-time decision. I had to let go of my old life as a woman with two legs repeatedly—and reluctantly. I didn't shrink from the truth, but it was no easy matter to look it in the eyes either.

In my reinventions, I guess I naturally stayed within areas that fit my core of being, which seems to be the desire to teach and to be on stage. As I look back, I am amazed at how my many reinvention attempts all seem to refer back to that little 8- or 9-year-old girl I was in the 1960s holding class for the neighborhood kids in my basement and that 17-year-old who wanted to be a star. I grew up to be an educator, an advocate, a motivator, a counselor, a coach, and a public speaker—adult versions of that same little girl who believed she knew it all and had to let others know and that teenager who dreamed of being on stage.

So, as you can see, everything I've gone through and achieved has brought me full circle in a strange way. All of these factors together have come to define the new me. As such, I am now able to move forward and succeed more naturally. I am like a fish in the water, like a bird on the wing, like a cat climbing a tree.

Ultimately, my story became one of power and purpose, and I was able to create that story out of the broken pieces that were left after my life and dreams were shattered by illness and disability. This is how I know it is possible to author a new narrative—as many times as we need to.

I had to do this at those times when people "called me out of my name," when men rejected me, and when people made unfounded assumptions about my abilities, my intelligence, even my sexuality.

My refusal to allow my self-esteem to be murdered by negative thinking and self-defeating thoughts—whether they came from me or from someone else—connected me to a wellspring of power. Tapping into that source within, I aligned with my true self and dared life to not let me live it.

It has taken prayer, practice, and perseverance, but as I stand in the embrace of all of life's possibilities and impossibilities, my belief in myself is unshakeable.

I have come to know that life is a song worth singing.

And the song is mine.

No matter what others may say, do, and think, I know that I have the power to negate everything that doesn't serve or support my best self. I didn't need anyone's permission to define myself and who I was. It was in this process that I relearned the truth about myself: that I was powerful, beautiful, sensual, and purposeful. I learned to experience life from a position of strength and understand that I had as much a claim on the best that life had to offer as anyone else. And I began to understand that God had not abandoned me.

I also know that the wellspring of power I found within myself is in *everyone*, buried deep perhaps, but still available for those moments when they believe they can do no more and go no further. My life's mission, I have discovered, is about so much more than my holding my own in the universe. It is about revealing to others that place within themselves, that largely untapped source that fuels greatness and personal power.

According to one very wise saying, which has been attributed to various people, "What lies behind us and what lies before us are tiny matters compared to what lies within us."

In the more than four decades since my amputation, I have translated my shattered dreams into a clear vision—a vision of my living my life as a brilliant, gorgeous, talented, and fabulous amputee. My preamputation dreams of teaching and performing have not been lost—they have merely been altered. Even though I may have faced cancer and chemotherapy, lost a leg to amputation, been stigmatized by others, suffered sneers and jeers, faced discrimination, and experienced rejection from boyfriends, I never lost my desire to pursue my education in spite of the barriers, and I never lost my desire to champion on behalf of others whose voices may not be as loud as mine but who still need to be heard. Speaking on behalf of those of us who do not fit society's concept of "normal" has now become the platform on which I teach, sing, dance, and perform.

Over the years, to realize my vision, I often took jobs working for organizations that paid little because they were working on behalf of others with disabilities. I've also held better-paying full-time jobs so that

I could continue fulfilling my dream of building organizations that serve others.

In finding the "right" job or career to go with the "new me," there has sometimes been a struggle between my full-time professional career and my part-time "building a movement" and advocacy efforts. Although both are important in my life, a human being only has so much time and soul to give, and I've been stretched thin in both. My goal now is to continue building my organizations until they are self-sufficient and will allow me the opportunity to move beyond my full-time career and devote myself to them full time so that I can achieve all the goals I have for them.

Although I have accomplished a lot over the years, my journey has been full of twists and turns, and I still have a lot to do to reach my desired destination. There are still conferences I have yet to host, speeches I have yet to give, TV shows and news programs that don't know about my work, and so many people that I have not reached with my life-changing message and story.

I am now who and what I am meant to be and am doing what I am meant to do. I have committed faithfully to my current goals as shown by my years of struggle to achieve them and my current investment of both time and money in bringing them to fruition.

Achieving these goals is my life's work and mission—
my purpose and meaning—as Viktor Frankl defined
it.

I have no control over the outcomes of my efforts, but what is most important is that I faithfully do
my part to achieve them. As author Les Brown said,
"Shoot for the moon, and if you miss, you will still be
among the stars."

I've done that in my own life, and now my mission
is to help bring out the star in others.

> "Not everybody can be famous. But every-
> body can be great, because greatness is de-
> termined by service."

> —MARTIN LUTHER KING JR.

45

No Shame in My Game

"Nobody can stop you but you. And shame on you if you're the one who stops yourself."

—DAMON WAYANS

"Diamonds are nothing more than chunks of coal that stuck to their jobs."

—MALCOLM FORBES

Being black, female, and disabled sometimes caused me to be thought less of by others. Perhaps they thought I was supposed to be ashamed of who and what I was—and the truth is that I bought into that at times when I was experiencing low self-esteem, poor body image, and a lack of confidence. Because I had these perceived three strikes against me, many people, including myself, lowered their expectations of me and expected me to strike out in life.

At some point, however, I couldn't take those things as an excuse to be less. Instead, in reinventing myself, I changed how I viewed those "strikes."

"I am woman; hear me roar!" I imagined myself shouting to the world.

"Dis*abled*. That's right, *abled*!"

I changed the focus and decided that my "deficits" in the eyes of others were not going to stop me. Instead, somewhere along the way, I either consciously or subconsciously decided that I was going to do more than others expected. If I had a class on the third floor, I climbed each stair. If my audience for a speaking engagement was indifferent or challenging, I demanded their respect. If my social outings made others uncomfortable, I boldly did the electric slide. I stopped expecting the parking space at the front entrance and started parking in any available space. Instead of quitting school or stopping with a bachelor's degree, I went on for my master's degree. Then, when I didn't feel that was enough, I went on to earn my doctorate.

Ashamed of being black, female, and disabled? Please.

■ ■ ■

When I discovered my true passion and purpose, I knew I needed higher education and to publish a book to give me greater credibility. As a result, I worked for both. I knew that I must be able to speak clearly and hold the attention of an audience, so I developed the habit of reading aloud twice a day to practice my voice. I also work on things as needed to move forward toward my goals. For example, I practice in front of a mirror before I present in front of an audience, and this practice has paid off over and over. Because my chosen identity requires a positive outlook, I've had to drift away from those destructive types of people I discussed earlier. If I allowed those types of people to influence me on a regular basis, I would not be able to be the person I've chosen to be. Being immersed in such negative attitudes and words would destroy my positive personality. I knew that I could not let myself or anyone else stop me, and I took the needed steps to protect myself. I was not going to allow any shame in my game.

When we choose to reinvent ourselves, we need to find out what it takes to be who and what we want to be. Then we need to start adding those things to our life that help us succeed and deleting those things that prevent us from doing so.

While we cannot control or predict the outcome of our efforts, we can control our efforts. When we act to become who and what we want to be, we have already succeeded to a certain degree.

From the time I faced the trauma of cancer, chemotherapy, and amputation—along with their aftermath—until now, every step represents my resolve to take the very next step.

As I climbed upward, each achievement was the result of simply taking the next step and never stopping. That's why so much of what I attempt to convey to others is about taking each small step, regardless of fear, criticism, or cost. Unless you take that next step, all of the following ones will be missed as well.

My walk is to inspire people to believe they can do anything. That girl who pictured herself as a diva is still here, having gone from "Diva in Waiting" to "Disabled Donna" to "True Diva"—one who does not let the label "disabled" define her. Somehow, I constantly found the grit to climb the highest academic mountain before me, to stand on stage with stature and affirmation rather than with shame and pity, to represent those whose conditions need a voice, to always take that proverbial next step.

While others don't know all of my pain and struggles, they can see my accomplishments. The cancer is gone. The chemotherapy is gone. The cancerous leg is gone. Each year that I go back for blood work and a chest X-ray and find that the cancer has not returned,

I live a bit more proudly, more boldly, and more joyfully as a woman with one leg.

Even though the message I got from society through the media was that I was not sexy because I had a disability, I ultimately came to feel sexy again, residual limb and all. Am I sexy in a way that everyone considers sexy? Probably not, but is anyone? A person could look like Beyoncé, but some people would still prefer Katy Perry, and vice versa. It's just the way the world is, and that's a good thing. If everyone found the same person sexy and the same person unsexy, there'd be far more affairs than there already are. And far more lonely people.

■ ■ ■

Each year, I gain momentum. I transform the obstacles and defeatist attitudes I face daily by channeling my energies toward championing the rights of those with disabilities and educating those without disabilities. I was and am happy and honored to stand firm on my full leg and partial leg to speak in solidarity with those whose voices might not be as loud as mine but who still need to be heard. I truly believe that I was too young to die because I had too many things to do.

At speaking engagements, I often remind my audience that I still have two legs; it's just that they can only see one of them. With this knowledge, I stand in victory, and I hope through my writing, speaking, and life to empower, encourage, and engage others to do the same.

At the end of the day, the question and answer for me remain the same: "What's a leg got to do with it?"

"Absolutely nothing!"

My leg was just one piece of me, and my life now consists of thousands of other pieces that create the beautiful mosaic that is the new and improved me.

After all of my battles, I am still here. I drive, I fly, and I live. I am a stepper, and I am on my way, sometimes with a prosthesis, sometimes with a cane, and sometimes with both, but I am always on my way. Undeterred. Undefeated. Still defiant. Here I stand. Maybe with only one leg that you can see. But I walk on, still moving forward and always—always—shooting for the moon.

No, there is no shame in my game. No shame at all.

> *"We must let go of the life we have planned, so as to accept the one that is waiting for us."*

> —JOSEPH CAMPBELL

Top to bottom: Graduation day from The George
Washington University (May 21, 2006).
Modeling shoots (2002, 2004, and 2006).

Top to bottom: Me on a motorcycle for a magazine article (2006).
Bold Beauty Project by photographer Shawn Mickens (2015).

Above: Photo of me taken for my LEGGTalk website.

Above: Photograph taken by Paul Morse
for Raw Beauty NYC (2014).

Appendix: My Twenty-Five Principles for Resilience and Reinvention

Although I know there is no one-size-fits-all solution for people experiencing crises and trying to reinvent their lives, I also know that the solutions that help one person can also apply to others. We are all human and suffer in much the same way. I have adopted the following twenty-five principles for helping *me* live *my* life and cope with the many changes and challenges *I* have faced over the years. I hope they are also beneficial to you in your effort to reinvent yourself.

1. Discover your meaning in life, and live with purpose and passion.

Who are you? What is your place and purpose in life? What do you want others to think and say about you when you pass away? Are you living in a way that will bring this about? Until you discover your meaning in life, you will be living without direction. Until you discover your passion, you will be living without fuel. If this is the case, you'll end up going in the wrong direction—or going nowhere. No matter what it takes, find your purpose, and the rest will follow.

In addition, strive to always keep your passion alive. You will not love *every aspect* of whatever you do, so try to find ways to spend more time doing the parts of it you are passionate about and to avoid the parts that you dread. You will do best those things you have passion for.

2. Be authentic (sing *your* song, not someone else's).

If you are now considering reinventing your life, there's a good chance that it is because you did not choose your life as it is now. It might have been imposed on you by circumstances out of your control, it might have been something others intentionally or unintentionally pushed you into, or it might have been a choice that you made and now realize was a mistake.

Yes, be willing to listen to the advice of others, but then analyze that advice and make the final decisions about your future yourself. You are in the best position to know your situation, what you want out of life, and what you are passionate about. A lot of people's lives have been ruined because they blindly followed the advice of others. Don't let this happen to you.

3. Don't wait for a "perfect" time and situation to start.

Many of us think that we have to wait for the perfect conditions to move forward in our life and career. We have to have the perfect office, fully stocked; the best computer system; a full staff; a complete and impressive portfolio; and/or a $250,000 loan. The truth is that many great businesses and organizations have been started in imperfect conditions. Steve Jobs, for example, started Apple in his parents' garage, and Mark Zuckerberg started Facebook from his college dorm room. If you wait for the perfect time and situation, you will never succeed. As Zig Ziglar said, "You don't have to be great to start, but you have to start to be great."

4. Do the work.

Dream about your future, and set goals, but don't *just* dream and set goals. Make them a reality by doing the work. This includes developing good habits that will bring you closer to success.

5. Get the education or training you need.

This doesn't necessarily mean you have to get a doctorate like I did. For you, this could mean job training or self-education. Find out what education or training you need to achieve *your* dream, and make sure you get it.

6. Find a mentor or a good role model.

If we have a mentor or role model who already has experience in a field we are interested in, we can often avoid a lot of learning by trial and error.

7. Recognize that you have the power to overcome obstacles.

I sing James Brown's song "Super Bad" each time I reach a milestone, big or small. When I graduated from walking with a walker to using crutches, I shouted, "I am bad." When I graduated from walking with crutches to using a cane, I shouted, "I am super bad." And when I learned to walk with my prosthesis for the first time, I shouted, "I am super super bad." When I earned my bachelor's degree, master's degree, and doctorate, I considered myself "absolutely super bad"! Having a positive attitude toward yourself and knowing that the power to overcome and succeed lies within you will enable you to confidently deal with anything that blocks your way.

8. Develop your strengths.

Analyze yourself to discover your strengths, and then develop them further. What are you good at? What do you like about yourself? Either fix or forget about your weaknesses; don't dwell on them.

Many people with disabilities learn to adjust to the world without all of the things other people have.

People who are born without arms, for example, learn to do things without arms and hands. Some develop the flexibility in their legs that allows them to use their feet for activities people usually do with their hands. They drive with their feet, write and type with their feet, and even eat with their feet. Similarly, blind people learn to move through the world without eyesight. So, yes, you can often use your strengths to overcome your weaknesses.

9. Don't worry about the little things.

In his book *Don't Sweat the Small Stuff...and It's All Small Stuff*, the late Richard Carlson discusses how we often get upset about things that really aren't that important. The next time you have a situation that might evoke anger or require more patience, ask yourself if it really matters in the larger scheme of things. So many people spend their life energy worrying so much about insignificant things that they completely lose touch with the magic and beauty of life. Try to relax and stop stressing so much.

10. Carefully watch over your thoughts and words.

You are in charge of your attitude and can always improve it. Say no to negative thinking, catastrophizing, and overgeneralizing. Avoid self-defeating negative thoughts and words at all cost.

11. Avoid toxic people as much as possible.

There are lots of negative, critical people around. Don't listen to them, and definitely don't mimic them and thus become your own worst enemy.

Remember, some people will criticize anything. Critics have disparaged Danielle Steel's writing, yet she remains one of the best-selling authors of all times, having sold hundreds of millions of copies of her books. In addition, more than twenty of her books have been adapted for television. Good thing for her that she didn't let the critics control her life and career! Instead of being a multimillionaire today, she might be lying around her shack, crying.

12. Live by *your* value system.

Hold yourself responsible for living up to your values, not the values of others.

13. Affirm yourself.

Positive affirmations can help you achieve specific goals and keep you balanced mentally, physically, and spiritually. Don't be afraid to tell yourself, "I love myself completely as I am" or "I am now reinventing my life exactly as I want it to be." You might not get the job, the promotion, or the spouse you are dreaming of, but that doesn't mean you are not worthy of it.

14. Recognize that you have intrinsic value.

You don't have to be or do anything to earn it; it came with your creation.

15. Expect the best.

Your expectations can affect your performance. If you expect failure, you are more likely to fail. If you expect success, you are more likely to succeed. The best way to guarantee success is to work hard for it and expect it from yourself and others.

16. Don't give up.

Always persevere toward your goals, unless you have a valid reason to quit, such as finding that they no longer serve your purpose.

For those times you might feel like giving up, you'll have to find something that will help you keep going. It might be simple stubbornness. It might be that you have a family that depends on you. Or you might just care so much about what you want to be and do that you can't quit. We all are different and have our own motivators. What are yours?

17. Plant seeds and give them time to come to fruition.

Sometimes, like in my case, you might be surprised to find that the flowers you plant bloom many years later—after you've forgotten all about them.

18. Reward yourself for small and great accomplishments.

Don't wait for others to acknowledge your victories. Acknowledge them yourself!

19. Don't let "failure" bring you down.

Many now-famous and now-wealthy business-people "failed" in one or two or more businesses before they ultimately succeeded. Many writers couldn't sell their early books—until they succeeded with later books. Many painters painted canvases that ended up in the garbage before they reached success. I encourage you to look at many (maybe all) of your so-called "failures" as learning experiences.

I always say, "Just remember FIDO (**f**orget **i**t and **d**rive **o**n)." Will we even remember these "failures" if we ultimately reach our goals? Will they even matter?

20. Surround yourself with support, especially with people who are more knowledgeable than you in their area of expertise.

Whatever you become or do, you probably won't be good at or passionate about every aspect of it.

Find a team to help, either as volunteers or employees. Trying to do everything yourself will slow your progress and might even stop you from succeeding. And if you are trying to do something that you're not good at or passionate about, it will not allow you to shine.

21. Decompress from time to time.

We all need a break. It will help physically and mentally.

22. Practice detachment.

- Allow yourself and those around you the freedom to be as you and they are.
- Do not rigidly impose on others your idea of how things should be.
- Do not force solutions to problems; this only creates new problems.
- Avoid being attached to outcomes.

23. Regularly perform acts of kindness.

Many psychologists confirm that random acts of kindness have a subtle psychological effect on us, brightening a corner of our personality even if we are the only one who knows about them.

24. Pray and/or feed your spirit.

25. Know that you can reinvent yourself over and over again.

When we think of who and what we are, we sometimes think it is something that is set in stone—something we can't change. The truth is that we can change both our purpose *and* our identity. Shifting circumstances, new priorities, and changing ideals might reveal a new purpose for our lives that is very different from the one we were so sure of a few years ago. Everything we learn and experience might play a role in the development of a new, revised purpose and identity.

Even if we've already reinvented ourselves one or more times, if we are no longer who and what we want to be, we can reinvent ourselves again.

The metaphor of the broken pot and the mosaic made from its pieces might help clarify this point. Even if we've already been broken and have picked up the pieces to produce a beautiful life mosaic that we are happy with, we might one day decide that that beautiful mosaic no longer works for us. If so, we can take those broken pieces and rearrange them again into another beautiful mosaic.

Malcolm X, the staunch fighter for the rights of black people, is a great example of this. He reinvented himself several times over his lifetime. He was Malcolm Little, the petty criminal who did time in prison. Then he became Malcolm X, an influential leader in the Nation of Islam. And then he became El-Hajj Malik El-Shabazz, the mainstream Muslim. Whenever his life no longer worked for him, he reinvented himself, and the new him was in stark contrast to the old him. When he changed, he changed dramatically.

My friend Karen Howze is another example of this. As she prepared to change her career again, she wrote, "Each [career] has been unbelievable. But [I] hope that this fourth reinvention will be as spectacular as the first, second, and third!"

Malcolm X and Karen both show that life is growth and change. Circumstances change. We change. We develop new desires. We can, and should, change our mosaic as often as it serves us to do so, reinventing and recycling ourselves over and over if necessary. There is something liberating in knowing that. Is there not?

If you live by these twenty-five principles, or even just several of them, it should help you reinvent yourself and become who and what you want to be. Keep in mind, however, that positive change takes time. At the same time, we must work for it with the faith that it can and will be achieved.

About LEGGTalk, Inc.

LEGGTalk's mission is to motivate and empower individuals to conquer their personal limitations (real and perceived) and achieve their visions of success.

At LEGGTalk, we strive for a world in which all people are treated with dignity and respect, can actively define their own lives, and can ultimately achieve economic freedom. Individuals with and without disabilities who are in transitional phases of their lives confront a myriad of issues and are at a greater risk of failure due to multiple challenges, including but not limited to underemployment, lack of accommodation, outward abuse, discrimination, and self-imposed isolation. We recognize these disparate disadvantages that systemically infiltrate our institutions and are committed to helping people overcome them.

SERVICES

LEGGTalk provides **L**essons of **E**mpowerment for Achieving **G**oals and **G**reatness through:

- **Public speaking:** Dr. Walton easily connects with her audiences, uplifting them with her signature "dream, reach, win!" messages and empowerment principles. With zeal and humor, she shares her principles for achieving success and life fulfillment, presenting motivational messages that connect with a range of audiences.

- **Workshops:** For personal or career enrichment, Dr. Walton provides one-on-one coaching and group workshops. These workshops are available to schools and institutions that understand the long-term benefits of developing and motivating their students and employees. Sessions are customized to participants' needs but mainly focus on helping them embrace positive living principles, identify their strengths, and create a strategic action plan to get them on a path to success.

- **Diversity training:** Workshops are also available that focus on bridging barriers between individuals with and individuals without disabilities by exploring negative attitudes and behaviors that undermine service to people with disabilities in workplace experiences. LEGGTalk provides disability awareness and sensitivity training, workplace guidelines for accommodating people with disabilities, and disability competency training.

- **Empowerment Salons:** The Empowerment Salon is a series of workshops, meetings, and conference calls in which women with and without disabilities can participate. It helps participants increase their self-esteem and enhance their self-image. Women with and without disabilities are able to network with one another to increase awareness of disability-related issues while promoting inclusion within society. Participants learn and acquire skills that are useful in their everyday lives.

Acknowledgments

I am grateful to God for sparing my life and allowing me to serve as a living testament to life's many miracles.

I am so fortunate to have many friends, old ones and new ones, who have inspired me to go for it!

A special thank you to Vanda Payton, who has been a loving friend and confidante since I was 11 years old.

I am proud to know folks like Sharon Graham, who has walked alongside me for more than forty years and continues to do so today.

Thanks to John Bing for reinforcing Proverbs 4...and reminding me that I do not have to play down my success for the comfort of others.

And to Vincent Jones, who knows the pain in choosing the right word.

Thanks to Alia Udhiri and her mom, Cynthia, who listened to me rehearse my speeches over and over again, for many hours. I understand it was painful for you.

Thank you to the boyfriends who walked out of my life to allow others to enter who could see past my one leg.

Much gratitude to Ms. Geraldine Harper, my junior-high-school homeroom teacher, who fueled my passion to write.

Special thanks to Erica Butler, Heather Watkins, Phoebe Goodson, Zazel O'Gara, and Cherri King for helping me create a platform where women of color who live with disabilities can raise their voices loudly and unapologetically.

To Mark Harris, I am most grateful for your penchant for photography and being drawn to photograph me in 1977. Your photographs remain with me today.

A multitude of thanks to Rick Bowers for the many years he remained a loyal servant to my story and for the countless hours he spent editing my words into this book.

About the Author

Donna R. Walton, EdD, is a survivor of osteogenic sarcoma, a life-threatening bone cancer that resulted in the amputation of her left leg at the age of 18. Since then, she has fought to overcome low self-esteem and rebuild her world, discovering new happiness and success along the way. The founder and CEO of LEGGTalk, Inc., and The Divas With Disabilities Project, Walton is an award-winning speaker who helps individuals and businesses fulfill their full potential. She also has more than a decade of experience in disability employment services, including her tenure at the Equal Employment Opportunity Commission.

The culmination of her life works earned her an invitation to the White House in 2014 to serve as a subject matter expert on accessibility and inclusion for the Office of the Chief of Operation Services' (OCOS) Working Group. Overcoming what Walton considers "triple jeopardy" to get to where she is today, she continues to live by the motto "What's a leg got to do with it?"

Articles by or about Walton have been published in several publications, including *HealthQuest*, *inMotion*, *Amplitude*, and *Disability Quarterly*. *Shattered Dreams, Broken Pieces* is her first book.

Walton continues to enjoy the journey of reinvention in Miami, Florida, where she currently resides.

For more information, visit www.leggtalk.com and www.divaswithdisabilities.com.